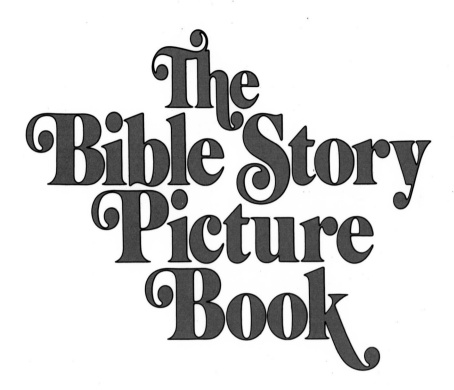

The Bible Story Picture Book

Compiled by ELEANOR L. DOAN

G/L REGAL BOOKS

A Division of G/L Publications
Glendale, California, U.S.A.

Grateful acknowledgement is made to Ethel Barrett, Lois Curley and Margaret Self of the Gospel Light Publications staff for their editorial help and assistance in preparing this manuscript.

OTHER G/L REGAL STORYBOOKS FOR CHILDREN

It Didn't Just Happen by Ethel Barrett

The Living Story of Jesus (Matthew · Mark · Luke · John)

Printed in Hong Kong

Published by
REGAL BOOKS DIVISION, G/L Publications
Glendale, California 91209, U.S.A.

Library of Congress Catalog Card No. 73-152801
ISBN 0-8307-0093-5

CONTENTS

OLD TESTAMENT

NEW TESTAMENT

FOREWORD

Someone has said, "The best way to get a child to eat his food is to let him see his parents enjoying theirs."

When I was a child in China we had an old Chinese Amah by the name of Wang Nai Nai—a gentle, homely old soul whom we children adored. Her favorite book was an old paperbound copy of the Bible. In fact, she had taught herself to read just so she could read the Bible for herself. It was not until I was grown that I was told of the evil life she had lived before she became a follower of the Lord Jesus. All I knew was that she loved this Book. And that she was one of the kindest, gentlest people I knew.

Each morning when I went downstairs to breakfast, my father—a busy missionary surgeon—would be sitting reading his Bible. At night, her work behind her, my mother would be doing the same.

Anything that could so capture the interest and devotion of those I admired and loved the most, I reasoned, must be worth investigating. So at an early age I began reading my Bible and found it to be, in the words of the old Scotsman, "sweet pasturage."

I didn't understand all I read. But that was not important. John Ruskin once said, "Whenever you read a book, go to the author to get his meaning." I went to the Author and I learned that the whole Book was about a people gone astray like lost sheep and about a Shepherd who gave His life to bring them back. And I was one of those sheep. My earliest recollections are of amazement and deep gratitude that He should love me so much.

Each morning in our home in China we had family prayers, reading verses aloud. (We all cut our teeth on the Bible.) Sunday nights when Daddy had finished his hospital rounds there were Bible games: "Go Till You Guess," "Twenty Questions," "Spit in the Ocean" (I never learned the origin of that name!) and others. They were fun; and they taught us a lot of Bible facts.

It wasn't surprising that when we went to North Korea to high school, the subjects I loved the most were the Bible classes. And later when I went to the States to attend college, I decided to major in Bible. At that time my heart was set on returning to China as a missionary. As it turned out, God had other plans.

Someone has well said that God never wastes his child's experiences. For what I learned in all the secular courses in high school and college was important, but what I learned from the Bible was vital!

In 1967 Petrus and Ernestine Ramoboa digging their 20-foot-square claim in Lesotho, South Africa, unearthed a diamond the size of an egg. It was eventually bought by the New York jeweler, Harry Winston, for $649,600. At the time of his find, Mr. Ramoboa had $4.00 cash. "Today," LIFE MAGAZINE reported, "he (Petrus Ramoboa) is rich, a personage, a fresh-eyed traveler in a world full of wonders." This is even more true of the one who with all his heart searches the Scriptures for the riches stored there: verses of comfort, verses of guidance, verses of reassurance, encouragement, correction—all we need for whatever we might be going through! For as has been said, "The Bible is the heart of God in the words of God." It is our one sure guide in an unsure world.

I have said all of this because if we want our children to love the Word of God, we must love it and read it for ourselves. If we want them to come to know God and to enjoy Him we must delight ourselves in Him.

Three-points for a good storyteller to follow also apply to teaching the Bible to our children—"Learn your story. Love your story. Live your story." If we want our children to love the Bible, we must learn the Bible, love the Bible and live the Bible.

When our children were quite small we started telling them Bible stories. We tried also to keep Sunday as a very special day on which they were allowed to have cokes, candy and chewing gum. (We limited these treats as far as possible to this one special day. This was partly to make up for the things which they were not allowed to do on Sunday. We have become more lenient in later years and I do not think it has been to their advantage.) Anyway, back to those early years when our children were small, we had Bible coloring books, Bible puzzles and Bible games. Sunday afternoons we spent together as a family, and by eliminating the games or occupations which we would do on other days of the week, we had more leisure to spend together studying the Bible and learning about God.

How I would have loved to have had a children's Bible story and picture book such as this one. For sheer drama and excitement there are no stories to compare with those of the Bible, and to have them presented so attractively is a tremendous asset, to families today.

Daily family worship is vitally important. I think the family should be called together by the father whenever possible. In our home, with my husband away most of the time, I have had to do this. I think especially when there are boys in the family it is unfortunate to always associate prayers with the mother. We have tried to make up for this when my husband is home. Family prayers are always so much more interesting and more relevant when he conducts them.

I believe it is important to keep the Scripture reading and prayer relatively brief and to vary it from time to time. Occasionally we have taken turns reading verses. At other times we have read through a book a few verses at a time. Or we have used a story to illustrate some spiritual truth. Usually the one conducting devotions leads in prayer, but at times such as in the evenings or on Sundays when devotions can be longer, it is good to have short prayers so each one in the family can take turns praying. Here again, be brief.

Bear in mind the words of Isaiah 28:10, "Whom shall he teach knowledge? and whom shall he make to understand doctrine? them that are weaned from the milk, and drawn from the breasts.

For precept must be upon precept, line upon line, here a little, and there a little." Start young and give it in small doses. For "a child's mind," said John Trapp in the 17th century, "is like a small necked bottle: pour in the wine too rapidly and much of the liquid spills over and is wasted."

One of the most personally delightful and rewarding things one can do is to memorize verses or passages from the Bible. What has been tucked away securely in the heart can never be taken away. Not only that, but at night when sleep is hard to come by, or in the day when busy with the dishes, or when driving a car, one can go over Bible verses and delight in their treasures. Even more, selections from God's Word are a deterrent to sin. We are told in Psalm 119:11, "Thy word have I hid in mine heart, that I might not sin against thee."

If your child is facing a particularly difficult situation, or has a special problem, select a verse that will fit that particular situation or problem and help him to memorize that verse. If you have a worrier, for instance, try "In nothing be anxious but in everything by prayer and supplication with thanksgiving let your requests be made known unto God. And the peace of God, which passeth all understanding, shall keep your hearts and minds through Christ Jesus." And a good one for boys is Proverbs 1:10, "My son, if sinners entice thee, consent thou not." Teach them also such basic verses as John 3:16; 14:1-6; I John 1:9; I Corinthians 13; Joshua 1:8; Psalm 1; 23.

But as soon as possible, launch them on reading the Bible for themselves.

We know that salvation is a miracle of grace. But the greatest thing which we as parents can do for our children is to delight ourselves in God and in His Word, putting it into practice with His help and faithfully teaching it to our children. "Line upon line, precept upon precept, here a little, there a little."

He will take it from there.

Ruth Bell Graham
Montreat, North Carolina

OLD
TESTAMENT

GOD MADE ALL THINGS

The Bible tells us wonderful things God did in the beginning.

Long, long ago there were no people. No animals. No flowers. There was nothing to see. Nothing to touch. There was only quiet darkness everywhere. But there was God! And God planned a wonderful world for us. God saw all the darkness. Then God said, "Let there be light." And there was light! God called the light daytime.

Part of the time God let it be dark. He knew we would need time for rest and sleep. God called the dark nighttime.

Again God spoke. This time He made the sky. And He made water—lots of water—for oceans and lakes and rivers and streams.

In between the water God made dry land. There were high mountains and round hills and big fields of dry land.

Just think, God made all these things! He made trees and bushes, and flowers and grass; and good things to eat like apples and potatoes.

But God was not finished. He made the warm sun to shine in the day. He made the moon and the twinkling stars to shine in the night.

Then God planned for all kinds of fish to swim in the oceans and lakes and rivers. He made birds. He made *all* living things—tiny creatures like the bugs and worms, and great big ones like elephants and giraffes.

The world was like a lovely garden. God looked and saw all the things He had made for our world. **2** And God said, "It is good." GENESIS 1:1-10

What do you see in this picture of things that God has made? Let's look outside. What do you see that God has made?

How glad we are that God has made our wonderful world! Let us thank Him for all things He has made. Let's pray quietly and briefly right now.

Thank You, God, for things I see.
Thank You, God, for loving me.   Amen.

GOD MADE
TIMES AND SEASONS

STORY 2

In the beginning God made a promise. God promised that daytime would always come after nighttime. "Day and night shall not cease," God promised us in the Bible. Over and over again we will have day, then night. We know this is true, for God keeps His promise.

God promised something else, too. God promised that we would have seasons. God planned the summer season with warm days. And God planned a winter season with cold days. "Summer and winter . . . shall not cease," God promised us. Over and over again we will have summer, then winter. We know this is true, for God always keeps His promise.

What do you do when it is summer? Do you go barefooted? Do you go on picnics? We like to play outside in the summertime.

After summer we always have fall. We know that it is fall when cool winds blow the yellow and red and brown leaves down, down, down from the trees. Fall means winter is coming soon.

What kind of weather does God send when winter comes? Is it cold? Does it rain? Does white snow cover the houses and trees and streets? Do you wear warm sweaters and mittens when you go outside in winter? We are glad for warm clothes and warm houses in wintertime.

After winter we always have spring. We know that it is spring when we see new leaves growing on the trees and flowers growing in our garden. Spring means summer is coming just as God promised.

4   GENESIS 1:11-18; 8:22

God made everything. He made time and He made seasons.
Look at the picture. Is it a daytime or a nighttime picture? Can
you tell what season it is?

Daytime is for work and play. Nighttime always follows day.
After summer comes the fall. God has planned and made it all.
After winter comes the spring with God's gifts of growing things.

Thank You, God, that I can see these gifts
of love You made for me.   Amen.   **5**

GOD MADE FAMILIES

Was God finished making our world when He made day and night and summer and winter? Oh, no! For God had more important plans.

The world God made was very beautiful. And there were many living and growing things. But there was no one—no people in all this wonderful world—to talk with God! There was no one God could love. And no one to love God.

So God made a man. He called him Adam. Adam was God's friend. They talked together many times. Then God made a woman so Adam would not be alone in this beautiful world. Adam named her Eve.

And God gave to Adam and Eve the loveliest garden home in all the world. God loved Adam and Eve. But God knew that Adam and Eve needed someone to love and care for.

So after they left their garden home to live in another part of the beautiful world, God sent them a baby boy. They named him Cain. Now there were three people in this family.

Cain grew and grew. Then God sent another baby boy to Adam and Eve. They named him Abel. Now there were four people in this family God planned.

God wanted families to be happy so He gave us some rules. God says to mothers and daddies, "Parents, love your children. Teach them to obey." God says to children, *Obey your parents*. God loves you. He wants you to have a happy family. You can help to have a happy family.

6   GENESIS 1:26-30; 2:7,18,21-23; 4:1,2.

How do you know God made each one in our family? In the
Bible we read, *All things were made by Him* (John 1:3). Who
is in the family God has planned for you?

Right now we can say thank you to God for our family.

Thank You, God, for my family.
Thank You, God, for loving me.   Amen.   **7**

GOD GAVE
WORK FOR ALL

Adam and Eve were happy in the garden home God made for them.

One day God gave work to Adam. "You will take care of this garden home, Adam. You may eat all the food that grows here—except the fruit from one tree." So Adam took care of the lovely garden and ate the good food, just as God had said.

God had a special work for Adam. He wanted Adam to give names to all the living creatures in the garden. So Adam gave names to all the animals. He gave names to all the birds.

Adam and Eve were very happy obeying God and working to care for their garden home. But one day a very sad thing happened. Adam and Eve ate some fruit from the one special tree God had told them not to touch! They had disobeyed the Lord God. They had sinned.

God loved Adam and Eve very much, but He had to punish them for disobeying. They could no longer live in their lovely garden home. Before God sent them out of their garden home, He made soft, animal-skin clothes for them.

Then He sent them out of the garden. Now Adam and Eve worked hard to plow the ground and plant the seeds to grow their food. They had much work to do. Cain and Abel helped their mother and father.

God has work for mothers and daddies to do. God has work for boys and girls, too. They all do good work because they love the Lord God.

GENESIS 1:26,29; 2:15,19,20; 4:2.

God has work for us to do. What work can you do? Let's show without talking what work we can do to help. I will guess what you are doing.

We want to be good workers because we love God. Let's ask God to help us do good work at home and at school. **9**

STORY 5　**GIVING FIRST CHOICE**

In Bible times a man named Lot and a man named Abraham lived with their families in big tent-homes. Lot and Abraham had hundreds and HUNDREDS of cows and sheep and camels.

Everyday Lot's helpers and Abraham's helpers took the animals to find green grass to eat and cool water to drink. But after awhile the helpers could not find enough grass and enough water for ALL those animals.

"This is OUR place!" Lot's helpers said to Abraham's helpers. "We saw this place first!"

"Oh, no you DIDN'T!" Abraham's helpers shouted. "We have as much right here as you do!"

Abraham and Lot heard about this trouble. "We cannot have our helpers quarreling," Abraham said to Lot. "We must move away from each other so there will be grass and water enough for all our animals."

Abraham and Lot walked up the hill. They looked all around. "YOU may have first choice of the land," Abraham said to Lot. "Take what you want for your family and animals."

Then Lot pointed to the good land nearby, where there was plenty of grass and water. "I'll take THAT land," he said. So Lot took his family and helpers and animals to the good land nearby. And Abraham took his family and helpers and animals to live in a land faraway.

The Lord loved Abraham and helped him have the land he needed. Abraham loved and obeyed the Lord. Abraham did what was right and good when he gave first choice to Lot. GENESIS 13:5-18

10

God was pleased that Abraham did what was right and good when he gave first choice of the land to Lot.

Can you give first choice of the cookies? Can you give first turn on the swing? When you give first choice—that is right and good. Then you are obeying God's Word!

Dear God, we want to obey You. Help us remember to give first choice to others. In Jesus name.   Amen.

VISITORS
TO A TENT-HOME

Abraham and his wife Sarah packed their tents and all their things. They loaded up the camels and traveled with their helpers and all their animals to a land where there was grass and water and trees to shade their tent-home.

Abraham and Sarah had much gold and silver. They had HUNDREDS of sheep and cows and camels. They had many helpers to care for them.

One day, Abraham saw one, two, THREE men coming toward him. Abraham knew how to be kind to visitors. So he hurried to them and said, "Please stay with us awhile! My helpers will bring you water. You may rest in the shade of our trees while I get food for you."

Abraham called helpers to bring water for the visitors. Then, he said to Sarah, "Please make cakes as soon as you can!" And Sarah did. Next, Abraham said to a helper, "Cook this meat the very best you can!" And the helper did.

Soon everything was ready. Abraham served his visitors a de-LICIOUS dinner of meat and cakes and butter and milk.

Before the visitors left, one of them said to Abraham, "You and Sarah will soon have a baby!" Abraham knew this would come true. For the visitor who said this was the Lord Himself!

Abraham and Sarah loved and obeyed the Lord. They were GLAD that the Lord was a visitor in their tent-home. They were so glad for the Lord's promise to send them a baby boy.

GENESIS 17:16-19; 18:1-16

Abraham and Sarah loved God. They were kind to three visitors.

The Bible says, *Be . . . kind one to another* (Ephesians 4:32).

This is what Abraham and Sarah did. What can you do to be kind to the little friends who come to play with you? What can you do to be kind to the grown-up friends who come to our house?

Can you remember what the Bible says? *Be . . . kind one to another.* Let's say it together.

A THANKFUL FAMILY

Abraham and Sarah lived a long time in their big tent-home. And then ONE day, Abraham and Sarah had their own baby boy—just as the Lord promised them! They named their baby Isaac.

Isaac grew and GREW—just as you are growing. When Isaac was big enough to walk and run and play like you do, his father Abraham said, "We will have a party so our friends will come and be glad with us for our boy Isaac!"

Sarah and her helpers were oh-so-busy getting everything ready for the party. Sarah helped little Isaac put on his very best clothes. And when it was time, fathers and mothers and children came to the party all dressed in their best clothes.

Everybody was glad to see what a fine big boy Isaac was. He had grown from a tiny baby to be almost as big as you are now. Many of the friends came to the party with presents for little Isaac. It was just like a birthday party!

Some of the friends came riding on camels from their homes far away. And some of the friends came walking from their tent-homes nearby. Abraham and his helpers brought cool water to their friends. Sarah and her helpers served them fruits and milk and meat and cakes—just all KINDS of good food! What a happy time everyone had when they came to see Isaac!

Oh how glad Abraham and Sarah were for their little boy Isaac! How they LOVED him! Again and again they thanked the Lord for sending Isaac to their family.   GENESIS 21:1-8

14

What did Abraham and Sarah say to God for sending Isaac into their family? What did they do to let their friends be glad with them? Did you ever go to a party like that?

Mothers and fathers love their children and sometimes give them a birthday party. Aren't we glad that we can show love for each other?

Thank You, God, for my family who love me.
Thank You for letting me love them too.   Amen.   15

STORY 8 # A WILLING HELPER

One day Abraham said to his most important helper, "Go to the faraway land where some of my family live. There you will find the girl whom the Lord wants my boy Isaac to have for his wife."

To find just the right girl could be hard to do. But the helper was glad to obey. The helper knew the Lord would help him do as Abraham said. So the helper loaded up the camels and rode away to find the right girl to be Isaac's wife.

Finally, the helper came to a well near the place where Abraham's family lived. There the helper prayed, "Lord, help me know who is the right girl to be Isaac's wife."

Very soon a lovely girl came to the well. She came to fill her big pitcher with water. "Please, would you give me a drink?" the helper asked her. Right away she gladly gave him a drink. And she even brought enough water from the well for ALL the helper's camels, too!

"Maybe THIS is the right girl!" the helper thought. And he gave her a ring and bracelets.

"My name is Rebekah," the girl said. "You may stay at our house!" And the helper did! Rebekah's family was kind to Abraham's helper.

"May I take Rebekah with me to be Isaac's wife?" the helper asked. Rebekah was glad when her family said yes.

The helper was glad, too. The helper thanked the Lord for helping him find the right girl to be Isaac's wife—just as Abraham had asked him **16** to do.   GENESIS 24:1-66

Abraham's helper was willing to do what he was told. He was glad to obey.

God wants us to be willing and obedient when we are asked to help. Will you do an errand for me? (Plan an errand for your child and discuss it with him.)

Maybe you can think of something else helpful to do. Sing the words, "This is the way I"; then hum the rest of the tune to *Mulberry Bush* while you act out what you plan to do.

A LONG TRIP ALONE

Have you ever gone on a trip? Did you ride in a car? In a train? Or in an airplane?

Jacob was going on a long trip. He was going to visit his uncle. And he was going to walk all the way by himself. Jacob's mother helped pack his clothes and the food he needed.

Then Jacob said goodbye to his mother and his father, and started off to see his uncle. Up hill and down hill Jacob walked all day. By the time night came, Jacob was very tired. He looked all around, but there were no houses, no motels where he could stay. He was all alone.

Jacob was so tired that he found a place to sleep right there on the ground. Jacob used a smooth stone for his pillow.

While he was sleeping, Jacob had a wonderful dream. In his dream Jacob saw a ladder reaching all the way from the ground to the sky. He dreamed that angels were going up and down the ladder. The most wonderful part of Jacob's dream was that he heard the Lord God at the top of the ladder say, "I am with you, Jacob. I will take care of you wherever you go." When Jacob woke up, he remembered what God had told him. Jacob was glad. He knew God would always be with him.

Then Jacob packed up his things. He walked and walked. Jacob walked all day. He walked step-step-step until he came to his uncle's house. And Jacob knew that God was with him all the way, in all places. For Jacob remembered God's promise.

18 GENESIS 27:43-46; 28; 29:1-14.

Let's pretend we are going on a trip. Where shall we go? Shall we go in our car? What shall we take with us?

The Bible tells about a boy who took a trip. God said to him: *I am with thee* (you), *and will keep thee* (you) *in all places* (Genesis 28:15).

Aren't you glad God loves us and is always near? I am so glad that His Son Jesus loves us too.

19

A BOY'S NEW COAT

In Bible times long, LONG ago, there was a boy named Joseph. He had one little brother, Benjamin. And TEN BIG brothers!

Sometimes Joseph stayed home and played with little Benjamin. Sometimes he helped his father and brothers take care of the woolly sheep.

One day Joseph's father called him into the big tent where they lived. And then he gave Joseph—What do you suppose? A beautiful coat! The most beautiful coat Joseph ever saw! It was purple and red and blue. And many more beautiful colors. "For me?" asked Joseph. And he put it on. "For ME? Oh THANK you, father!" And he ran down the path to show it to everybody.

One day Joseph's father asked him to go and find his brothers who were taking care of the sheep. Joseph ran to put on his new coat.

"When you find your brothers, Joseph, come back and tell me how they are," his father said. And off Joseph started down the road.

Joseph walked UP one hill and DOWN another. UP one hill and DOWN another. Then—

He met a man walking across the field. "Have you seen my brothers?" asked Joseph. "They are taking care of my father's sheep."

"I think you will find your brothers on the other side of that hill," said the man. So UP the hill and DOWN the other side Joseph went. And sure enough—there they were! How glad he was to find his brothers! Joseph was glad he could do this to help his father who loved him and gave

20 him a new coat.   GENESIS 37:3,13-17

God has given us many things from which to make our clothes. God has made wool on the sheep for sweaters and coats. God made the soft cotton to grow on plants so we can have cotton for shirts and dresses.

Do you remember to thank God for the clothes you have? Our Bible tells us, *Be thankful unto him* (God) (Psalm 100:4).

Thank You, God, for love and care,
Thank You, God, for clothes to wear.   Amen.

FOOD FOR A FAMILY

When Joseph grew to be a man, he did not live with his father and brothers. The Bible tells us that Joseph went to live far away. And there he became the king's very best friend!

The king gave Joseph beautiful clothes to wear, and a gold ring, and a gold chair. The king even gave him special horses. And a beautiful chariot to ride in, too.

Joseph was not only the king's very best FRIEND, he was, also, the king's very best HELPER! God helped Joseph know what to do. Joseph told the king's people to grow more and more corn and wheat, and to save it in big barns. Soon the big barns were packed FULL!

All the time he was the king's helper, Joseph did not forget about his father and his brothers far away. He thought about them. And he wondered how they were—if they had enough corn and wheat for all their families.

Then, one day—ten men came to Joseph's big barns to buy food. They came from the very same country where his father and brothers lived! These men told Joseph that they were brothers. And that their brother Benjamin was at home.

Right away Joseph knew that these men were HIS brothers. Oh, what a happy surprise!

Joseph gave them food to take home. And that's not all! He told them to bring back their father and brother Benjamin and all their families to live near him always. And they did!

That is how God helped Joseph have food for all his family. GEN. 41:39-49; 42:1-7; 45:1-13

How does God help our family have enough food? What food did we have this morning? This noon? For supper?

We should give God our thanks for the food He helps us to have. We can give thanks to God like this:

We thank You now, dear God in heaven,
For food and home today,
We thank You for Your love and care
In Jesus' name we pray.   Amen.

THE BABY
WHO WAS A SECRET

Can you keep a secret? Big sister Miriam kept a very important secret. Miriam helped keep baby brother a secret so the king's soldiers could not find him. For the king had told his soldiers to kill all Hebrew baby boys.

Baby Moses grew bigger and bigger. His voice became louder and louder. Finally his family could not keep Moses a secret any longer. "What can I do to keep my baby safe?" his mother wondered. God helped Moses' mother think of just the right thing to do.

She made a strong basket and covered the outside with sticky tar to keep the water out. Then she wrapped baby Moses in soft blankets and put him in the basket-boat.

When no one was looking, Miriam helped her mother carry Moses in his basket-boat to the river. Carefully they put the basket-boat down on the water. "Miriam, hide in the tall grass here and watch little Moses," her mother said. Then she went home.

Soon the king's daughter, the princess, came to the river. She saw the basket-boat in the water. When the princess saw baby Moses, she said, "I will keep him for my own baby!"

Miriam ran to the princess, "May I find someone to take care of this baby for you?" "Yes," said the princess, "I need someone to take care of him." Miriam ran and brought back Moses' own mother to take care of him.

Miriam and her mother knew the Lord God was their helper.   EXODUS 1:7-22; 2:1-10.

24

How did God help Moses' mother know how to save her baby? She knew the Lord God was her helper. How did God help sister Miriam keep the secret? She knew the Lord God was her helper.

The Lord God is our helper, too. The Bible says, *The Lord is my helper* (Hebrews 13:6). The Lord has ways for helping each one. How is He your helper when you play? When you are sick? When you are hungry? When you are on vacation?

What would you like to say to God for being your helper? **25**

VOICE IN
THE BURNING BUSH

One day Moses was out on the hills taking care of his sheep. Suddenly he saw flames of fire coming out of a bush. Moses went closer and watched the fire burn and burn. "How strange," Moses thought. "This bush is burning but it is not burning up." Moses came closer and closer to the burning bush.

"Moses, Moses!" a voice said. Moses was surprised. He did not see anyone.

But Moses answered. "Here I am."

"You are in the presence of God," the Voice said. Moses was frightened. This was the voice of God speaking from the burning bush.

"I am God. My people have prayed to me," God said to Moses. "I have heard their prayers, and I am going to help them." Moses listened quietly. How glad he was that God was going to help his people.

Then God said, "Moses, I have chosen you to lead my people to the land I have for them."

"Oh, no!" said Moses, "Not me! I do not know how to do such an important thing. The people would never follow me!"

Then God said, "Do not be afraid, Moses. I will help you know what to do."

Moses listened to the voice of God. God told him how to help his people. And Moses obeyed the words of the Lord.

Moses wrote the words God spoke to him. And Moses wrote how God helped him know what to do. In our Bibles we can read the words that
26 Moses wrote. EXODUS 3; 4:1-18.

How did God talk to Moses?

God talked to Moses from a burning bush. Today God speaks to us, too, but not the same way. How do you think God talks to us today?

The story of Moses hearing the voice of God in the burning bush is a true story because it is in the Bible, God's Word. The Bible says, *The word of the Lord is right* (Psalm 33:4).

We can believe what the Bible says. It is the way God talks to us.

GOD'S CARE

DAY AND NIGHT

Long ago in Bible times, God wanted His people to go on a long, LONG trip to a special land He had for them. So God spoke to a man named Moses. "You will lead my people," God said. "And I will tell you exactly what to do."

But what a time God's people had to get started! First, Moses went to the king and asked him to let the people go. But would the king let them go? He would NOT! He said "No!"

Moses went back again. And the king said "No!"

Moses went back AGAIN. And still the king said "NO!" But Moses went back more and MORE times. And finally the king said "Yes."

My! What excitement! How everyone hurried to get ready! Mothers cooked food and packed the clothing and blankets. Children filled the leather water bags. Fathers got out the horses and camels and donkeys. Everybody helped. They put bundles on the animals and on their own backs, too. And off they started on their long, LONG trip to the new land.

God's people did not have sign-posts, or road-maps to show them the way. But they DID have GOD! And do you know what He DID? He put a great big white cloud in the sky. And God's people followed it wherever it went.

When night came the cloud became bright as fire in the sky. Even in the dark they could see just where to go! The people saw the great cloud. And they knew that God was taking care of them night and day. EXODUS 3:7-10; 5:1,2; 13:17-22

28

God told Moses He would take care of the people on their long trip. Who are some of the people in the picture God took care of?

Let's pretend that we are going on a long trip. What are some of the things we must do to get ready? (Pack clothes, ask someone to care for pets, study maps, etc.) Can you think of something else we should do? We should ask God to take care of us. How do we know He will do this? We know He will take care of us because He loves us.

A PATH

THROUGH THE SEA

Yes, God was taking care of His people on that long, LONG trip to the new land. The big cloud was there in the sky for them to follow every day. And every night the cloud became bright as fire so they could see where to go.

God's people walked on and on and ON. And when they came to a big lake called a sea, God told them to stop and to camp.

Everything was going fine until—they saw soldiers! Soldiers were coming! Coming to take God's people back to the king's land! What WOULD they do now? If only there was some way to get across the sea! But there were no bridges. No boats. How COULD they get across? What would they DO?

"Don't be afraid," said their leader, Moses. "God has told me just what to do."

Sure enough, God HAD told Moses what to do. Moses stepped up to the very edge of the water. Stretched out his hand, and—what a wind there was! O-o-o-o- how it blew! It blew and BLEW until the water moved out of the way and made a dry path for God's people to walk right through the sea! Mothers and fathers and brothers and sisters and all the animals!

Finally, every one of God's people was on the other side. The king's soldiers were still coming. BUT—

Moses held out his hand again. And SPLASH! The waters all came back together. The king's soldiers could not get through, for God was

30   taking care of His people!   EXODUS 14

In Bible times God often took care of His people in wonderful and special ways. How did He take care of the people while they were traveling to a new land?

God helped His people because He loved them. God takes care of you in special ways, too, because He loves you. What happens when you get hurt? When you are sick? How good God is to give you Mother and Father and other special people to help you! You can say thank you right now to God.

WATER FOR

TIRED TRAVELERS

On their long, LONG trip to the new land, God took care of His people every minute.

So when the people became thirsty, they drank water out of the jars and water bags they carried with them. Of course, there were no faucets or drinking fountains along the way. And every time the jars and water bags were empty, God's people found water and filled them all up again. And then on they would go, following the cloud.

But ONE time—their jars and water bags became emptier, and EMPTIER. The people became thirstier and THIRSTIER. And they did not see water ANYWHERE!

On they walked in the hot sun. On and on and ON. The people were thirsty. Moses, their leader was thirsty. All the people, and all the animals became thirstier and thirstier. Then Moses said, "God is still taking care of us. Let's go on a little farther." So on and on they walked, until— "There! Up ahead! Trees! Lots of trees! Oh, hurry, hurry to those trees!"

And sure enough! Under the trees were wells of water—deep holes in the ground filled with cool, clear water. There were not just two or three wells. But there were one, two, three— TWELVE wells of cool, clear water!

Oh how the tired and thirsty people drank! They FILLED their jars and water bags with the cool water. The children laughed and splashed. How glad they all were to rest, and to drink the good water. They knew that God was still taking **32** care of them!   EXODUS 15:27

How many people in the picture are glad for the water? What does the daddy have on his back? What do you think he will do with the water?

What is the mother doing? Who is having a drink of cool water? Who is waiting for a drink of cool water?

Dcesn't a drink of cool water taste good when you are thirsty? Only God can make water. *God is good* (Psalm 73:1). The next time you drink water will you remember to thank God for it?

FOOD

FOR HUNGRY PEOPLE

The people walked on and on and ON to the land God had for them. And God kept right on taking care of them every minute.

Each time they stopped to cook their dinner, they used up a little more food. And a little more food. And a little MORE food. Until—one day, their food was nearly all gone!

"What shall we DO?" they said. "There is no place to BUY food."

And Moses said, "Don't be afraid. God sent a cloud to show us the way. He made a dry path through the sea. He helped us find water. And He is still taking care of us. You wait and see!"

So the people cooked the tiny bit of food they had left. They cleaned up the camp. And they went to bed. Then, in the morning—the ground was covered with little round white things that looked something like tiny biscuits! The mothers and fathers looked at these little white things. The boys and girls looked at them. They touched them. Then everybody tasted them.

"It's MANNA! It's good to EAT," the people said. "But what is it?" they asked Moses.

"This is bread that God has given us," Moses answered. "Take all that you need for your families. But take just enough manna for today!" And the people did.

The next day there was more manna. And the next day there was MORE manna. God never forgot to send manna as long as His people needed it. God was still taking care of His people on **34** their long, long trip. EXODUS 16:1-18, 31,35

God's people became very hungry as they walked on and on to their new land. But God promised to help them and take care of them. What is the special food the people in the picture are picking up?

Do you get hungry? Every day? What do you do when you get hungry? God never forgets to take care of His people. How has God taken care of you today?

WRITTEN ON STONE

The people were busy, busy, busy! For two days they were busy making their camp clean and ready. On the third day the people would hear God speak!

When the third day came, Moses told the people, "Come out of your tents and stand quietly at the bottom of this mountain." The people waited quietly.

Soon, the people saw bright flashes of lightning. They heard loud booming thunder. A great cloud came to cover the mountain. The people watched and listened.

Then God spoke to Moses. The people heard God's voice. His voice sounded like crashing thunder. "I am the Lord your God," God told the people, "Worship Me." Then God said something especially to the children. "Love and obey your father and mother."

God's great voice was so loud and strong that the people said, "Let God speak to you alone, Moses. Then tell us what God wants us to know."

So Moses climbed the mountain. Moses climbed and climbed until the people could not see him. There on the mountain Moses saw God's hand write the rules for His people.

Because God loved His people, He knew they needed rules to know what was right and good. God wrote ten rules on two big pieces of stone. God gave to Moses these two big pieces of stone with the ten rules on them. These rules are called commandments. In our Bible we read the rules **36** God gave to Moses. EXODUS 19:10—20:22.

God gave us His commandments so we would know what is right.

Let's read the Ten Commandments from the Bible (Exodus 20:3–17). These are rules that God asks us to follow if we love Him. What rule did God give especially for the children? What do you do to obey that rule? Does our family have rules to obey? What are some of these rules?

We show our love for God by obeying His commandments and we show our love for our family by obeying the rules.

37

LOVE GIFTS FOR
THE TENT-CHURCH

STORY 19

God's people walked and walked for many days on their long trip to the new land. God showed them when it was time to stop and rest. The families then set up their tents and camped until God showed them it was time to go on.

Moses was the leader of God's people. One day God told Moses to come up on a high mountain. On the mountain God talked to Moses. God gave Moses rules for making a tent-church.

When Moses came down from the mountain, he called the people together. He said to them, "God wants us to make a tent-church. We will call it the tabernacle. We will need many love gifts and many helpers to make this tabernacle."

God's people loved the Lord God. They were glad to bring their love gifts of gold, silver, pretty stones, cloth and wood. And God's people were glad to work together.

Zzz-Zzz went the saws as the helpers cut the wood for the posts and furniture. Bang, bang went the hammers as they pounded the gold and silver into lovely bowls and lamps. Tap-tap, tap-tap, went the hammers as the helpers cut designs in the wood. In-'n-out, in-'n-out, went the needles as the weavers made beautiful curtains of red and blue and purple threads for the tent-church.

For a long time the people worked to make the tent-church. At last it was finished. Moses thanked God for all the helpers who brought gifts and worked to make the tent-church a lovely

38 place.   EXODUS 25:1-9; 35:4-35

God told Moses to have the people build a special kind of of church. What was it? Yes, a tent-church! What did the people do to help make it a lovely tent-church? Pretend that you are helping the people build the tent-church. (Have child pantomime the sawing of wood, hammering, sewing curtains, pounding silver, etc.)

What can you do to help make our church a lovely place? Also, you can show your love for God by helping and taking love gifts to our church.

THANKFUL PEOPLE

Did you know that the very first thanksgiving time started long ago in Bible times—oh a VERY long time ago? Well it did.

Do you know who told the people to have a special thanksgiving time? God did!

"God has told us to have a special thanksgiving time," Moses said to the people. Then, Moses told them exactly what God wanted them all to do. And they did it.

This is what the people did. They cooked good things to eat. Every day for seven days. Roasted meat, bread, fruit, cakes, honey—oh just all the good food you can imagine!

Most of the people had ALL the food they needed. And SOME of the people had MORE than they needed. But some of the people did not have ENOUGH. So, do you know what? The people who had MORE food than they needed gave some to those who did not have ENOUGH! God asked His people to do this so it would be a happy thanksgiving for everybody.

And then the people cut branches from trees and bushes. With these they built little shelters. And the mothers and fathers and children lived in these shelters for seven days. At night they slept in their shelters. And they watched the twinkling stars in the nighttime sky. Oooh it was fun! Just like camping!

What a happy thanksgiving time they had! The children played together. Mothers and fathers talked together. Every day the people thanked

40 God together. LEV. 23:34-44 DEUT. 16:13-15

The Bible says, *It is a good thing to give thanks* (Psalm 92:1). Do you give thanks to God for the food He gives us at every meal?

Can you name some other good things God gives you? (Help child to think of clothes, home, parents' love, God's love, etc.) Can you thank God for the good things you have named?

Thank You, God, for taking care of all my needs,
Thank You, God, for loving me. In Jesus' name.   Amen.   **41**

BOAZ SHARES WITH RUTH

Did you ever have a friend who ate all his cookies and did not share them with you? How did you feel? The Bible tells us of some people who shared their—. Well, you listen to what they shared.

It was time to harvest the grain in Farmer Boaz' fields. His workers cut the grain and tied it into bundles. They were hurrying to get their work done. Some of the grain fell on the ground. But the workers did not stop to pick it up. Farmer Boaz told them to leave that grain for the people who did not have enough to eat.

One day Boaz saw a young woman picking up grain in his field. "Who is she?" Boaz asked.

"Her name is Ruth," the worker told Boaz. "She comes every morning to pick up grain. She shares it with her mother Naomi."

"I am glad to share my grain with Ruth and Naomi," Boaz decided. "I will help Ruth get all the grain she needs." Then Boaz said to his workers, "Be kind to Ruth. Drop a little extra grain where she will find it to fill her basket." And Farmer Boaz told the workers to share their water and lunch with Ruth, too.

When night came, Ruth went home to her mother Naomi. Ruth's basket was filled with good grain. Ruth told Naomi about the kind farmer, Boaz. Naomi was glad. Now they could make bread and little cakes to eat. Naomi and Ruth thanked God for the grain which Farmer Boaz shared with them. Boaz was glad, too, that he had shared.

42   RUTH 1:22; 2; 4:1-17.

The Bible says, *Share what you have* (Hebrews 13:16, Living New Testament).

Ruth and Naomi were happy because Farmer Boaz shared his grain with them. Farmer Boaz was happy, too, because he shared.

Are you happy when a friend shares something with you? How do you feel about sharing with a friend? With someone in your family? With visitors? What do you have that you would like to share with someone?

HELPING
STORY 22 **IN THE TENT-CHURCH**

"Samuel, you are big enough now to be a helper," his mother said. "You are big enough to go to the tent-church and help Eli, the minister."

Eli was happy Samuel came to be his helper. Every day Samuel swept the floors and polished the lamps. He opened the church doors in the morning and closed them at night.

One night Samuel heard a voice calling, "Samuel, Samuel."

Quickly Samuel jumped out of bed and ran to Eli. "Here I am, Eli," he said.

"I did not call you," said Eli. "Go back to your bed now." And Samuel obeyed.

Soon he heard the voice calling again. Samuel got out of bed and ran to Eli.

"Here I am. You called me," Samuel said to Eli.

"I did not call you," said the old minister. "Go back to your bed, Samuel." And Samuel obeyed.

Soon the voice called Samuel again, "Samuel, Samuel."

When Samuel ran to Eli this time, Eli knew that it must be the Lord God Who was calling. "Go back to bed," said Eli. "When the voice calls again say, 'Speak, Lord. I am listening.'"

Again Samuel went to bed. When the voice called again, Samuel said, "Speak Lord, I am listening." Samuel listened carefully to all that God told him.

Samuel obeyed the Lord God and was a glad helper in the tent-church. For Samuel loved the Lord God and he always served *the Lord with gladness.*   I SAMUEL 1; 2:1-18,26; 3:1-21

44

How did Samuel help at the tent-church? He helped because he loved God. He was happy to be a helper and to
serve the Lord with gladness (Psalm 100:2).

Let's draw a picture of our church. Think of some ways you
can help at our church because you love the Lord. Let's write
them down so you can remember to do them.

Now you can learn the Bible verse that will help you do them
happily. *Serve the Lord with gladness.*   45

SONGS OF PRAISE

In Bible times there lived a boy who loved to play his harp and sing. While he took care of his father's sheep, he played his harp and sang his own songs. This shepherd boy was David.

David watched his sheep carefully. He watched so they would not get lost or hurt while they were climbing the steep hills.

David practiced using his sling while his sheep were resting. David had to be ready with his sling to protect his sheep from wild lions and bears.

Sometimes David stayed all night on the hillside with his sheep. These were happy times for David. He watched the moon and the stars in the nighttime sky and he sang his own songs of love and thankfulness to God. David played his harp so well and sang his songs so beautifully that the people called him the sweet singer of Israel.

One day while David was taking care of his sheep, a messenger came. "We need someone to play sweet music for our king," the messenger said.

So David went to live at King Saul's palace. When the king felt sick and unhappy, David sat beside the king and played his harp softly. King Saul often felt much better when David sang and played for him.

We can read many of David's songs in our Bibles. We can sing many of the songs David wrote, too. These songs are called psalms in our Bibles.   I SAMUEL 16:14-23; 17:34-37.

46

David often made up songs and sang them while he was taking care of his father's sheep. What were the songs about?

Can you think of a glad song you would like to sing to tell the Lord you love Him? Let's be like David and make up our own song to tell God of our love. You sing your song first and then I'll sing it with you. Then you can sing the song for others as a thank-you to God.

HELPING A FRIEND

David lived in King Saul's palace. He sang and played songs on his harp for the sick king.

At the palace David's best friend was Jonathan, the king's son. David and Jonathan promised to be loving friends. Jonathan gave David his strong bow for shooting arrows. He gave David his beautiful coat and belt, too. Jonathan gave David his best things to show that David was his friend.

David played and sang for the king but the king did not get better. One day the king was so sick he tried to hurt David. David had to leave the palace and hide from the king.

Jonathan went and found his friend David. "I will do anything to help you," he said. Then Jonathan and David promised again that they would always be friends.

"I will go," Jonathan told David, "to find out if my father, King Saul, really wants to hurt you. Then, in three days I will come back here," Jonathan said. "If I shoot some arrows a little way, it means it is safe for you to come back to the palace. If I shoot them a long way, you must go far away."

When Jonathan came David saw him shoot the arrows a long way. David knew this meant he would have to leave his friend, Jonathan. Jonathan said to David, "Even though you leave, I will always be your good friend."

And just as the Bible tells us David and Jonathan were friends who showed their love at all **48** times.   I SAMUEL 18:1-4; 20:35-42.

David and Jonathan were friends. How was Jonathan a helpful friend? We are obeying God's Word when we are helpful friends. The Bible says (read and point to these words in your Bible, then let child read and point to them): *A friend loveth at all times* (Proverbs 17:17). What does "at all times" mean? What can you do to help your friends all of the time and not just when you want to?

OBEYING GOD'S WORD

David hurried to find a place to hide from King Saul. David and some of his helpers found some big dark caves up on a mountain. There they decided to stay and hide.

King Saul and his soldiers looked and looked for David. One day David saw the king coming. "Hide in the cave!" David called to his men. "King Saul is coming with his soldiers."

Quickly David and his men ran far back inside the cave and hid in the dark shadows. Closer and closer the king and his soldiers came. King Saul came into the cave and stopped to rest. He took off his long coat and laid it on the ground in the cave. Saul did not know David and his men were watching him from their hiding places in the cave.

David slowly moved toward the spot where the king's coat lay. Quietly, carefully, David cut off a big piece from Saul's long coat. Then slowly David crept back into the dark cave.

Soon, King Saul picked up his coat and walked down the mountain path. David waited until Saul was at the bottom of the mountain. Then in a loud voice, David called to Saul, "See this piece from your coat? I was close enough to hurt you, but I did not!"

Now King Saul was ashamed of himself for wanting to hurt David. "May the Lord give you many good things because you did not hurt me today," King Saul said to David.

Because David loved the Lord God, he did what was right and good. He obeyed the Word of the Lord.

50   I SAMUEL 24.

What is David doing in this picture? David knew that King Saul had been unkind and wanted to hurt him. What did David do that was right and good?

When is it hardest for us to be kind? It is hardest to be kind when someone is unkind to us. What do you think is the right thing to do when someone is unkind to you?

STORY 26 KEEPING A PROMISE

David was the new king now. Saul and his son Jonathan were dead.

David always remembered his dear friend Jonathan. One day David thought about his promise to be kind to all of Jonathan's children.

David wondered how he could keep that promise. "Did my friend Jonathan have any children?" King David asked an old servant of Jonathan's family.

"Yes, Jonathan had a son named Mephibosheth," the servant told David. "His feet were hurt when he was a little boy. He is grown up now. But he is lame. It is hard for him to walk."

"Find Mephibosheth," King David commanded his servants, "and bring him to me."

The servants soon found Mephibosheth. "We have come," they said, "to take you to King David. He wants to see you."

When Mephibosheth came into the beautiful palace, King David was waiting to see him.

"Because I loved your father, Jonathan, I want to be kind to you," David said to Mephibosheth. "I want you to come and live with me. I will give you everything you need."

And so lame Mephibosheth came to live with the king. David remembered his promise to be kind to Jonathan's son, Mephibosheth. David treated Mephibosheth just like one of his own sons. Because he loved the Lord, David kept his promise to Jonathan. David did that which was right and

52   good.   II SAMUEL 9:1-13.

After David became king he remembered a promise he had made to his friend Jonathan. What was that promise? Can you find someone in the picture who was a part of King David's promise? How did King David keep his promise?

When you make a promise do you keep it? What promise did you make to Mother? To Father? What did you do to keep your promise?

BIRDS FEED ELIJAH

Can you think of ways God helps you and your family have food? God gives us our food, doesn't He? The Lord is good to us all.

God had a special way of giving food to His helper Elijah. The Bible tells us that Elijah loved and obeyed God. God told Elijah to live by the little brook Cherith. "There you will have water to drink," God said. "And I will take care of you. I will send food to you every day," God told Elijah.

Elijah obeyed God. He went to live by the brook Cherith. There were no houses, no stores, no people by the brook. "Where will I get food?" Elijah wondered. He remembered what God had promised. So Elijah just waited.

Soon Elijah saw big birds flying around. Closer and closer they came. Could it be? Yes, the big birds were bringing meat and bread to Elijah, just as God had promised! Every night and every morning the birds came with food for Elijah. And there was always water for Elijah in the brook Cherith. God took care of Elijah just as He had promised. I KINGS 17:1-6

For all around me everywhere
There is so much to show God's care;
So many good things I can see
That tell He loves and cares for me.
I am so glad that I can say
"I thank Thee, Lord, for food today."

54   —Author unknown

Can you name the man in the picture? The birds are ravens.
God sent the ravens with something He promised Elijah. What
was it?

God does not send birds to give us our food. How does
God help us have our food? (Discuss how seeds are planted,
how they grow and how they produce food which is taken to
stores for families to buy.)

What do we always do before we eat our food? Do you say
thank you to those who buy and fix your food?   **55**

FOOD FOR A FAMILY

In Bible times a mother and her little boy lived in a land where it did not rain for a long LONG time. Because it did not rain wheat could not grow in the fields.

One day this mother had only enough wheat flour and oil to make a few flat loaves of bread. There was no more wheat flour or oil after that was gone.

A minister came by and asked the mother, "May I have a drink of water, please? And may I have a little bread, too?"

The mother wanted to help the minister. "But I have only enough wheat flour and oil to make bread for supper tonight," the mother said.

"Please, make bread for me," the minister said. "Then make bread for your family. The Lord God has said He will give you all the wheat flour and oil you need."

The mother gladly mixed the wheat flour and oil that she had. She patted out the bread dough and baked it. She gave it to the minister.

When it was time to make bread for her family the mother had a happy surprise. She looked in the flour jar. There WAS enough wheat flour! She looked in the oil jug. There WAS enough oil! As long as she needed it, there was enough flour and oil to make bread for her family—and for the minister, too!

How thankful she must have been that God helped her—in this SPECIAL way—to have food for her family. She was glad she had food to share with other people, too! I KINGS 17:8-16

Look at the picture. Who was glad to have food to share?
Helping others is a way to show love for the Lord Jesus.

There are places in our world where people do not have
enough food. Do you know of any places where people do not
have enough food? How can you help others to have food?
(Guide thinking to include praying for people, giving money to
help hungry people, helping missionaries who work where
people need food, etc.)

GOD'S GIFT OF WATER

Were you ever very, very thirsty? Did you ever need water, and not have any? The Bible tells us about some people who needed water. It had not rained in their land for a long, long time.

The people of that land did not love and obey the Lord God. Instead, they prayed to gods they made out of wood and stone.

Elijah lived in this land. One day the Lord God gave His helper Elijah a special message for the king. Elijah said that God would send no rain in this land for a long, long time, for the people did not love and obey God.

Just as God had said, no rain fell. No fruit grew on the trees. The corn did not grow in the fields. Not one thing grew.

The ground was brown and dry. The rivers and lakes dried up. People were hungry and thirsty. Animals were hungry and thirsty.

Elijah went to the king again. "When your people love and obey God, I will pray for rain." So Elijah called the people together. The people watched and listened to Elijah tell them of the Lord God. Then they believed and worshiped the Lord God!

"Now God will send rain again," Elijah said. And off Elijah ran to pray and watch for the rain God had promised. Soon there was a small cloud away off in the sky. "Rain is coming," Elijah said. Soon there was much rain. There was water enough for everyone.

The people knew that God sent the rain. They **58** gave thanks to the Lord. I KINGS 17:1; 18:41-46

What was it like when there was no rain upon the earth? There was only one Person who could give rain upon the earth. Who is that Person? God provided water as a part of His loving care.

Do we need water? How do we use the water God sends? Let us bow our heads right now and thank God for sending water to Elijah and the people, and for sending rain upon our earth.

JARS AND JARS OF OIL

In Bible times there lived a mother who did not have any money. She did not have money to buy food or clothes for her family. She did not have money to pay what she owed other people.

One day a man said to the mother, "Pay the money you owe me! Or, I will take your two boys away to work for me."

The mother hurried to the minister Elisha. "What shall I do?" she asked. "I have no money to pay the man—only a little pitcher of oil."

"Borrow all your neighbors' empty jars," Elisha told her. "Then, pour the oil from your pitcher into the empty jars." So the mother sent her boys to bring all the jars they could borrow—big jars, little jars and medium-sized jars.

The mother began to pour the oil from her little pitcher. She poured and poured and POURED! (All the time God was making more and more oil!) The boys brought more and more jars. Their mother poured more and MORE oil —until there were no more empty jars!

Then the mother hurried to tell Elisha this wonderful thing that had happened. "I poured the oil from my pitcher—just as you told me. Now we have jars and JARS of oil!" she said.

"Sell your oil, and pay the man what you owe him," Elisha told her. "You will have money left to buy what you need."

Again and again the mother and her boys must have thanked God for Elisha's help. Elisha was glad that God had showed him how to help this

60 mother and her boys! II KINGS 4:1-7

Elisha was a glad helper. God showed him how to do many good and kind things for people. Can children do good and kind things? Who are two good helpers in this picture? Who are the glad helpers at our house? Are you a glad helper?

Would you like to tell ways you are a glad helper by playing out what you do? Can you show what you do to thank God for His help?

ROOM ON A HOUSETOP

In Bible times a minister named Elisha often came to tell the people in Shunem about God. A kind woman and her husband lived in Shunem. They often asked Elisha to come to their house to eat and rest. Elisha was glad to eat with these kind friends and rest at their house.

One day after Elisha had gone, the kind woman said to her husband, "Elisha is a good minister. He goes many places telling people of God. Let us make a special room for Elisha upstairs on the flat roof of our house. And whenever he comes to visit us, he can go to his own room upstairs to rest and pray."

The husband thought this was a good idea. So he called the builders. The builders came with their hammers and saws and wood. Schzz-schzzschzz went the saws. Bambambam went the hammers. And before many days, the room up on the flat roof was all finished!

The kind woman and her husband hurried to put a bed and a chair in the new room. They put a table and a lamp in the room, too.

Soon Elisha came again to visit this kind family. They could hardly wait to show him the new room. Step-step-step up the stairs Elisha went with the kind woman and her husband.

What a happy surprise for Elisha! "This room is for you, Elisha!" the kind family said.

Many times Elisha rested in this room and said thank you to these kind friends. And many times he must have said thank You to God for these **62** kind friends. II KINGS 4:8-13

Elisha was a minister who went everywhere helping people. Some friends in Shunem were kind to Elisha and invited him to their house. What did they do for their company?

Isn't it fun to have company come—and stay overnight at our house! How do you help Mother get ready for the friends who are coming? The Bible tells us that one way to show love for the Lord is to help our friends have a happy time at our house (from I Peter 4:9).

PRAYER TO HELP FRIENDS

Elisha often visited the kind friends who made an upstairs room for him. "You are very kind to me," Elisha told the kind woman one day. And then Elisha told her some specially glad news! "I know you would like to have a child. God will send a baby boy to you and your husband."

When their baby was born, the kind woman and her husband were VERY glad! They loved their baby. They took care of him as he grew and grew.

Then one day, the boy became sick—so VERY sick. His mother held him and rocked him. She did everything she could to make him well. But the boy died.

Quietly the sad mother carried her boy up-up-up the stairs to Elisha's special room. Gently she laid the boy on the bed. She told her husband she was going to find Elisha.

"Oh, PLEASE! Please, come with me!" the kind woman begged Elisha. And Elisha went to help this woman who was always so kind to him.

Elisha went up-up-up the stairs to his room. On the bed was the dead boy. Elisha went into the room and shut the door. Then he prayed. Elisha prayed that God would help this kind family by making their boy live again.

Suddenly, the boy sneezed. He opened his eyes! The boy was alive! "You may come and get your boy now," Elisha called to the mother.

The happy mother thanked Elisha for asking God to help her. Elisha was glad that he could **64** help by praying for his friends. II KINGS 4:11-37

Elisha loved his friends in Shunem who invited him to stay in their home. What did he do for them?

Do you ask God to help your friends? Do you thank God for the friends who help you? God is glad to hear His children pray. He sends the answer that is best because He loves us. Your friends and your family are glad when you say *I will pray for you unto the Lord* (I Samuel 7:5).

TELLING A SOLDIER

The Bible tells of a little girl who lived with Captain Naaman and Mrs. Naaman. The little girl took care of Mrs. Naaman's pretty clothes. She combed Mrs. Naaman's long black hair. Every day she helped Mrs. Naaman in many ways.

One day Mrs. Naaman was sad, very sad. "WHY are you sad?" the little girl asked Mrs. Naaman.

"I am sad because Captain Naaman is sick with terrible sores. And no one in all our land can make him well," Mrs. Naaman answered.

"Oh, I wish Captain Naaman would go to the minister Elisha!" the little girl said. "The Lord has helped Elisha make OTHER people well."

When the sick captain heard what the little girl said, he hurried to Elisha's house. Elisha told the captain, "Wash yourself in the river seven times!"

At first the captain did not want to wash in that muddy river. Then, slowly he walked into the water. One, two, three, four, five, six—SEVEN times he went down under the water. When he came up THIS time, he looked at his arms and his hands. He looked at his legs and his feet. Every ONE of his terrible sores were gone. The LORD had made him WELL!

Right away Captain Naaman hurried to thank Elisha and show him the wonderful thing the Lord had done! Then, the captain hurried home. Everyone was SO glad to see him well again. The little girl was ESPECIALLY glad she had told the Naamans about the wonderful ways the Lord helps and shows His love.

66 II KINGS 5:1-15

Who is the little girl in the picture? What did she do to help
Captain Naaman? Did she tell what the Lord had done?

You can help your friends by telling them about the Lord
Jesus. And, you can thank the Lord Jesus by praying this
prayer:

Thank You for the great and loving things You have
done for me. Help me remember to tell my family and
friends about these great things. In Jesus' name. Amen.

67

LOVE GIFTS
FOR THE TEMPLE-CHURCH

For many years God's people came to worship the Lord God at the beautiful temple-church. They brought love gifts to keep the temple-church clean and beautiful. Then somehow they forgot the temple-church was the house of God.

The walls of the temple-church became cracked and broken. The floors and furniture were dusty and dirty. The red, blue and purple curtains were torn. The temple-church was dirty.

King Joash saw the cracked and broken walls of the temple-church. He saw the dust and dirt on the floors and furniture. He saw the torn curtains. Because King Joash loved the Lord God, he was sad to see the house of God broken and dirty.

Then the king told the minister, "Have a big box made with a hole in the top. Then put the big box by the door of the temple-church."

When the box was finished, King Joash told the people, "We will make the house of God clean and beautiful again. Bring your love gifts and put them in the big box at the temple-church."

And many people brought their love-gift money. Soon there was enough money to pay workmen who fixed the broken walls and furniture. Sewing workers made lovely new curtains, while others cleaned and polished.

When the temple-church was clean and beautiful again, King Joash called the people to the temple-church. How happy they were that their love gifts helped to make their temple-church a lovely place to worship God!   II KINGS 12:4-15

68

Why did King Joash ask the people to bring love-gift offer-ings to the temple-church? Why do we take love gifts to our church? How do our love gifts help at our church? Name something in our church which you think your love-gift money helps to buy.

People can do other things to make God's house clean and beautiful. Guess what I am doing to help. (Act out ways to help—arrange flowers, bring offerings, etc.) Now let me guess what you are doing to help.

GLAD TIMES
IN THE TEMPLE-CHURCH

King Hezekiah knew what God's Word said on the big scrolls. Hezekiah wanted his people, also, to know what God's Word said. He told his people to come to the temple-church where they could worship God and learn what God's Word said.

In the temple-church the minister read God's Word from the big scrolls. Helpers sang songs of love and praise to God. Other helpers played trumpets to praise the Lord.

One day King Hezekiah sent letters to all the cities where God's people lived. "Come to the temple in Jerusalem," the letter said. "Come with your families and stay seven days."

How happy the boys and girls were as they planned their long trip with their mothers and fathers and their grandmothers and grandfathers.

At last the day came for the families to start on their trip to the temple-church in Jerusalem. Up hill and down they walked until they came to the beautiful temple-church.

Every day for seven happy days boys and girls, mothers and fathers, grandmothers and grandfathers worshiped God in the temple-church. Every day they heard ministers read God's Word from the big scrolls.

When seven days were over, the people said to King Hezekiah, "We do not want to go home yet. Let us stay a little longer." So they stayed one, two, three, four, five, six, seven days longer! What a happy time God's people had worshiping God together in the lovely temple-church.   II KINGS 18:1-7; II CHRONICLES 31

King Hezekiah asked the people to bring their love-gift
money to the temple-church. What else did he ask them to do?
Act out some things the people did and see if I can guess.

When the people went to the temple-church they were to
hear the word of the Lord (II Kings 20:16). This is what the
Bible says we should do in church. Let's pretend we are reading the Bible (make hands like book) and repeat what the
Bible says: *Hear the word of the Lord.*   71

A KING'S PRAYER
IN THE TEMPLE-CHURCH

King Hezekiah was sad. For a messenger had come to tell Hezekiah that a wicked king with many soldiers was coming to fight God's people. The big army could hurt the people. The army could break down the walls of Jerusalem.

When the messenger had gone, King Hezekiah called his helpers and told them to build two strong walls around Jerusalem. Then Hezekiah said to his people, "Do not be afraid of the wicked king. He has only his many soldiers to help him. We have the Lord God to help us."

Soon a messenger from the wicked king brought a letter to Hezekiah. In the letter the wicked king said, "I am coming with my big army to capture you and your people."

Hezekiah went to pray at the temple-church. He asked God to help and protect his people from the army of the wicked king.

Then Hezekiah received good news from Isaiah, the minister. Isaiah had a message from God. He said, "Do not be afraid, Hezekiah. God heard your prayer in the temple-church. God will not let the wicked king's army hurt the people."

God protected King Hezekiah and all the people. And everyone knew that it was the Lord God Who saved King Hezekiah and the people. The people from faraway lands heard how God saved His people from a king with a big army.

The people brought love gifts to the temple-church. And they thanked God for hearing the king's prayer and helping them.

Look at the picture and tell what King Hezekiah is doing. When King Hezekiah prayed in the temple-church, what did he ask God to do? Does God always hear His children pray at church? At home? At play? At school? Where else does He hear them?

> We can talk to God in the nighttime;
> We can talk to God in the day.
> For God hears all His children
> And answers when they pray.   Amen.

BUILDING
THE TEMPLE-CHURCH

One day King Solomon said to the people, "Let us build a church more beautiful than our tent-church. Let us build a temple-church where we may worship God."

King Solomon then chose many workers to build the new temple-church. The stone workers cut and cut big pieces of rock to make smooth blocks. They pulled and pulled the big stones up the hill. Then they fitted the big stone blocks to make the outside walls of the temple-church.

The wood workers cut big cedar trees in the forest and sawed them into boards. They used knives to carve beautiful designs in the wood for the inside walls of the temple-church.

The painters covered the inside and outside of the temple-church with bright shining gold.

The sewing workers made beautiful curtains of red, blue and purple threads. On the curtains the workers sewed designs of flowers and angels with gold thread.

Then the ministers carried special furniture from the tent-church into the new temple-church. They carried in beautiful new gold and silver bowls that the metal workers had carefully made.

When all was ready, King Solomon called the people to come and worship God in the new temple-church. The people played horns and harps. They sang praises to the Lord God. The people were very happy for their new temple-church. II CHRONICLES 3; 4; 5; 6:1-21

74

What did King Solomon do so the people could worship the Lord God? Who were some good helpers in the house of the Lord? What did they do? (Encourage child to tell or act out answers.)

In Bible times when the people went to church they said, *This is the house of the Lord* (I Chronicles 22:1). When we go to our church we can say this, too. Let's bow our heads and thank God for our church. (Let child express his thanks to God.)

STORY 38   A BIBLE SCROLL FOUND

"It's time to clean the temple-church," King Josiah told the people. So the helpers polished the lovely bowls and candlestick. They dusted and swept. Until—away back in a dark corner, the minister found something. Something very important. It was the Word of God written on a big Bible scroll.

When the minister found this Bible scroll he said to the helpers, "Quickly, take the Bible scroll to King Josiah."

"Look!" the helpers said to King Josiah, "The minister found the Word of God away back in a corner of the temple-church."

"God's Word!" said the king. "Read it to me now so I will know what God said." The helpers read God's Words on the Bible scroll. King Josiah listened. Then he sadly said, "We have not obeyed these words of God."

King Josiah then sent a message for all the people to come to the temple-church. He wanted his people to hear God's Word. Mothers and fathers, boys and girls, grandmothers and grandfathers came to hear God's Word at the temple-church. The people listened and listened while the king read from the Bible scroll.

Then King Josiah said to all the people, "Today we will make a promise to God. We will promise to obey His Word."

Mothers and fathers, boys and girls, grandmothers and grandfathers all stood up. And together they promised, "We will love the Lord **76** and obey His Word."   II CHRONICLES 34

When the Bible scroll was found in the temple-church, King Josiah asked a minister to read God's Word. All the people listened to the Word of God. Why was King Josiah sad when the Bible scroll was read? What did the people promise to do?

Do you remember to obey God's Word? Can you say *I will not forget Thy* (God's) *Word* (Psalm 119:16)? Ask God to help you to remember God's Word and to obey it.

GOD'S WORD

READ AND OBEYED

One day Ezra said, "I would like to go to the big city of Jerusalem where many of God's people live. There I can teach the Word of God." So Ezra went to ask the king, "May I go to Jerusalem and teach the people what God's Word says?"

"Yes, Ezra," said the king. "You may go. You may take with you all who want to learn God's Word." And he gave Ezra a love-gift offering to take to the temple-church in Jerusalem.

Then Ezra sent a message to God's people. "I am going to Jerusalem to teach the Word of God. If you want to go with me, meet me by the river and we will travel together."

Quickly mothers and fathers, boys and girls, grandmothers and grandfathers packed clothes and blankets and food. Then they met Ezra, who prayed to God to help them on their trip.

When the people reached Jerusalem, they brought their love gifts to the temple-church. And they thanked God for taking care of them.

One day Ezra told the people in Jerusalem he would teach them what God's Word said. Many people came to hear him. But when the people heard God's Word they were sad. They knew they had sinned for they had not obeyed God's Word. "God loves you. He forgives you when you are really sorry for your sins," Ezra told the people. "Tell God you are sorry. Show God you love Him by doing what His Word says."

How happy the people were to know this! They listened and obeyed God's Word because
78   they loved God. EZRA 7-10; NEHEMIAH 8; 10:39

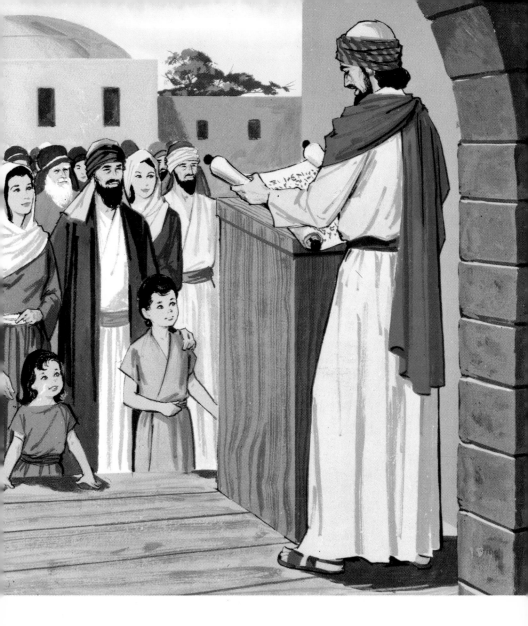

What is Ezra doing in the picture? When the people knew they had not obeyed God's Word, what did Ezra tell them they should do? Do you only listen to the Word of God, or do you do what it says? You can show God you love Him by doing what He asks you to do in His Word, the Bible.

Thank You, God, for our Bible. Help us to do what You ask us to do in Your Word. Amen.

WORKING TOGETHER

Nehemiah lived in the palace with the king. He was the king's special helper.

One day Nehemiah's brother came from far away to visit him. Nehemiah was glad to see his brother.

"Tell me about Jerusalem, the city where our people used to live," Nehemiah said.

"Jerusalem is not beautiful now," said the brother sadly. "The strong wall around the city is broken. And the houses are falling down."

When Nehemiah heard this he was very sad. Because Nehemiah loved the Lord, he wanted to help. He prayed, asking God to help him know how he could help the people build the walls and the houses in Jerusalem again.

When the king knew Nehemiah wanted to go to Jerusalem, the king said, "You may go and help the people build the wall. Come back when it is finished."

Nehemiah was very happy. He thanked the king and started on his way to the far away city.

When Nehemiah reached Jerusalem he called all the people together and said, "Let us build our city again. First we will build the wall. Who will help?"

Everyone wanted to help. The people were glad to do their part. Bang! Bang! Bang! went the hammers. Every day they worked. And soon the great wall was finished.

Nehemiah was glad he could please the Lord God and help the people build Jerusalem.

NEHEMIAH 1; 2; 3:28; 4:6; 6:15; 8:1-8.

How did Nehemiah show he loved God? And how did the people show they loved God? (Let child comment.) Let's pretend Nehemiah has asked our family to help him rebuild the wall. What will each one do to help?

Thank You, God, for this Bible story about Nehemiah and the people who showed they loved You. Help us remember to show our love to You by working happily with our family and friends. In Jesus' name.   Amen.   **81**

TELLING A KING

The Bible tells about a king who had a special dream one night. When the king woke up, he could not remember his dream. "Tell me my dream," the king told his wisemen. The wisemen thought and thought. But no one could tell the king his dream.

The king was VERY angry. "All of you will be killed—unless you can tell me the dream!" the king told the wisemen.

One of the king's wisemen was named Daniel. He said to the king, "Please wait a little longer, O King. I will soon be able to tell you the dream."

Daniel knew that NOBODY—nobody in all the world could tell the king his dream. Daniel knew that only the Lord God in heaven could help him know what the king had dreamed.

So Daniel hurried to some friends who loved and obeyed God. Daniel said to them, "Please, pray for me! Ask the Lord God to help me know the king's dream." So Daniel's friends prayed. And Daniel prayed that the Lord would help him.

Then—one night, the Lord God showed Daniel what the king's dream was! Daniel THANKED the Lord God! Then, Daniel hurried to talk to the king.

"O King, the Lord God in heaven has helped me know your dream. I can tell you now," Daniel said. The king was glad Daniel helped him remember his dream.

Daniel was ESPECIALLY glad he could tell the king of the Lord God Who helped him tell the dream.

82   DANIEL 2:1-30

One night the king had a dream. Daniel told the king his dream. How did Daniel know the king's dream? Who did Daniel talk about when he told the king his dream?

What can you tell your friends about the Lord God? Name several friends you can help know the Lord and love Him. Perhaps you can invite your friends to go to Sunday School with you so they can learn more about the Lord and His Son, Jesus.

TELLING MANY PEOPLE

In a faraway land there lived a man named Daniel. He loved and obeyed the Lord God. The king and the people of this faraway land did NOT love and obey the Lord God.

Daniel was the king's special helper. Some wicked men did not want Daniel to be the king's special helper. So these men asked the king to make a new rule that everyone should pray only to the king. Then the wicked men watched Daniel. Would HE pray only to the king, like the new rule said?

The very next day the wicked men saw Daniel praying to the Lord. They hurried to tell the king, "O King, Daniel has disobeyed your new rule. Today we saw him praying to his God!"

The king was sad. He liked Daniel. But the rule had been made, and all who disobeyed had to be punished. Sadly, the king put Daniel into the lions' den.

In the morning, the king hurried to the lions' den. "Daniel! Daniel!" he called. "Did the Lord to Whom you pray take care of you?" Would Daniel answer?

"I am not hurt," Daniel answered. "The Lord sent an angel to shut the lions' mouths." How glad the king was!

Then, the king made a rule that all his people should know of the Lord. The king sent letters everywhere to tell many kings and their people what the Lord had done! And this was the way MANY people in MANY lands learned about the Lord God.

DANIEL 6

The man in the picture is writing letters for the king. What did the king tell his helper to write? Do you think Daniel was glad he had helped the king know wonderful things the Lord has done?

Can you tell your friends about the Lord? Can you tell them He loves them, too? What else can you tell them about the Lord? A Bible verse to learn is, *Tell . . . great things the Lord hath done* (from Mark 5:19).

NEW
TESTAMENT

GOD'S PROMISE

Do you know what a promise is? A promise means you will do what you say, doesn't it?

The Bible tells us of the most wonderful promise ever made. God promised that one day He would send a wonderful Saviour and King to earth. The people waited many, many, many years for God to keep His promise. Some people even thought that God had forgotten about His promise.

One day God sent an angel to a lovely girl named Mary. Mary loved the Lord God. She knew about God's promise to send a Saviour and King to earth. How surprised Mary was when the angel came and told her, "God has chosen you, Mary, to be the mother of a wonderful baby boy This wonderful baby will be God's own Son," the angel told her. "You will call His name Jesus."

One day Mary and her kind husband Joseph went to the little town of Bethlehem to write their names in the king's book. It was nighttime when Mary and Joseph came to Bethlehem. There were many other people who had come to Bethlehem, too. And there was no more room left where Mary and Joseph could stay. There was only a place in the stable with the cows and donkeys. So Mary and Joseph stopped to rest in the stable.

That very night in the stable at Bethlehem Mary's baby was born. She called His name Jesus, just as the angel had said. For this little baby was the Saviour and King God had promised. For God so loved the world that He sent His Son, the Lord Jesus, to be the Saviour-King.

ISAIAH 7:14; LUKE 1:26-38; 2:1-7

What is a promise? Did you ever promise to do something special for someone you loved?

God made a very special promise to the whole world because He loved us so much. He promised a love gift for all people. Who came to be God's love gift for us all? What did the angel say His name would be? The angel said, *Thou* (you) *. . . shalt* (shall) *call his name Jesus* (Luke 1:31).

89

GOD'S BEST GIFT

One day Joseph said to Mary, "We must go to the city of Bethlehem! The king said that we must go there to write our names in his big book." So Joseph helped Mary get ready for their long trip.

Mary rode on a little donkey. And Joseph walked alongside. Cloppety-clop, cloppety-clop, they traveled for days and days. And finally— they came to Bethlehem!

It seemed that EVERYBODY came to write in the king's book. There were people EVERY-WHERE! EVERYTHING was crowded! There was just NO room for Mary and Joseph.

Finally, Joseph knocked on the door of an inn. "May we stay here?" he asked.

"No," the innkeeper said, "there's no room here. But wait—there's the stable for animals. You may stay there if you want to." And they did. They were so glad for a place to rest!

And there in that stable, that very night, God's promise came true! Yes! Baby Jesus was born! Mary wrapped Him in soft warm clothes. And she laid Him—oh so carefully—in a manger on the clean hay.

Mary called the baby's name Jesus, just as the angel had said. For this little baby was the Saviour and King God had promised. For God so loved the world that He sent His Son, the Lord Jesus, to be the Saviour-King.

LUKE 2:1-7

God kept His promise and sent the baby Jesus. Christmas is Jesus' birthday. Jesus is God's best gift to us.

Do you like to receive gifts? When you receive a gift what do you say? We want to say thank you to God for sending His Son, the Lord Jesus. (Let your child thank God for giving His best gift.) Can you learn this Bible verse? *He* (God) *loved us, and sent his Son* (I John 4:10).

THE
ANGEL'S GOOD NEWS

How do we find out when a new baby is born? Does someone call on the phone? Does someone write us a letter?

In Bible times some shepherds found out when a very special baby was born. And they found out in a very special way. This is how the shepherds found out.

They were taking care of their sheep on a hillside near the city of Bethlehem. Everything was quiet. It was nighttime. Then suddenly— there was an ANGEL! Right before their eyes! And there was a bright light in the sky! The shepherds couldn't believe it.

"Do not be afraid," the angel said. "I have good news! Jesus the Saviour is born in the city of Bethlehem! He is lying in a manger." The Lord Jesus! Could it be TRUE?

Just then the sky was FULL of angels. And they were saying, "Glory to God in the highest! On earth peace, good will to men."

Suddenly the angels were gone. The bright light was gone. And it was dark again. The shepherds looked at each other. It MUST be true! "Let us go NOW to Bethlehem and find out," the shepherds said. And they did! Run-run! Step-step! How they hurried! Until—

They came to the stable. There was Mary. There was Joseph. And there was a manger with a baby in it. The baby Jesus! It was true! Just as the angel told them. Shhhhh. Oh so quietly they came near to see this dear baby. And they **92** thanked God for baby Jesus. LUKE 2:8-20

It's exciting to hear good news, isn't it? And right away you want to know more and see for yourself if it's really true!

The shepherds heard some good news. What was the good news they heard? What did they do when they heard this good news?

Jesus' birthday IS good news! We want to share it, too. You can tell this good news. Can you name some friends you want to tell that Jesus is God's gift of love to everyone?

WISE MEN
STORY 46   FOLLOW THE STAR

In a far away country a long time ago, there lived some men who knew many important things. They were called wise men. These men knew of God's promise to send a Saviour-King. They knew God promised to send a special star when the Saviour-King was born.

One night the wise men saw a new bright star in the sky. No other star was as bright as this one. "A king has been born," said one wise man. "We must go and find Him," said another wise man.

The wise men packed their best gifts and started on their trip to see the Saviour-King. They rode a long, long time on their camels until they came to a big city. "Has a new king been born here?" they asked. No one in that city knew about the new king. Even the king of that city did not know about the baby God had sent. But the wise men were sure a special king had been born. For they had seen the bright star in the heavens. This star was the sign God had promised. Then someone remembered that long ago God had promised a Saviour-King would be born in the little town of Bethlehem. "We will go to Bethlehem," the wise men decided.

Now the bright star started to move. The wise men followed the star as they rode their camels down the road to Bethlehem. And there the bright star stopped over a house.

When they went inside the house they found Jesus with Mary and Joseph. They kneeled down and gave their precious gifts of love to Jesus, the

94   Saviour-King.   MATTHEW 2:1-12

The wise men said they knew of a special promise that God made long ago. What was it? Before the wise men started out to follow the star, what did they do? Who were the gifts for?

Giving these gifts to Jesus was the best way the wise men knew to show their love. What gifts of love can you give the Lord Jesus? Have you given Him your love? If you really love the Lord Jesus, tell Him you love Him right now.

GOING TO
THE TEMPLE-CHURCH

Baby Jesus was the special baby God sent from heaven. But only a few people knew this wonderful news. Of course, Mary and Joseph knew. And day after day they lovingly took care of baby Jesus! Then one day—

It was time to take baby Jesus to the temple-church! He was not as big as you are. He was much too little to WALK. He had to be CARRIED! For He was still a tiny new baby. Mary rode to the temple-church on a donkey. She held baby Jesus in her arms. Joseph walked beside her. It was a LONG way to the big temple-church.

When Mary and Joseph and baby Jesus got there, somebody was WAITING for them at the temple-church! Yes, a man named Simeon was waiting inside the temple-church. As Mary and Joseph came in with baby Jesus, RIGHT THEN AND THERE, Simeon knew that this was the special baby God had told him about.

Simeon was SO glad to see baby Jesus! He held out his arms. And Mary let Simeon hold baby Jesus. Right then Simeon THANKED God for sending the Lord Jesus!

Then, Mary and Joseph left two little birds at the temple-church. These were their special LOVE GIFT to thank God for giving them baby Jesus.

What a happy time it was when Mary and Joseph took baby Jesus to the temple-church! And they talked many, many times about this happy day.

LUKE 2:21-40

Simeon was happy to see the baby Jesus. He wanted to hold Him! What did Simeon do when he held baby Jesus? Joseph left two little birds at the temple-church. Why did he do this?

Simeon and Mary and Joseph all wanted to thank God for giving them the baby Jesus. Would you like to thank God, too, for the special baby He sent from heaven?

Thank You, dear God, for sending Jesus to us. In Jesus' name.   Amen.   **97**

TRAVELING TO A FARAWAY LAND

God helped Mary and Joseph take care of baby Jesus ALL THE TIME He was growing.

One time a very wicked king wanted to kill baby Jesus. So God sent an ANGEL one night while Joseph was sleeping. "Get up," the angel said to Joseph. "Take Mary and baby Jesus FAR away to the land of Egypt. There the wicked king cannot hurt Him!"

"Hurry!" Joseph whispered to Mary. "We must take baby Jesus away to the land of Egypt!"

And OH, how they did HURRY! They packed food and clothes! They wrapped little Jesus in soft blankets. Mary sat on the donkey and held baby Jesus close in her arms. They were ready to go! So Joseph led the way.

Shhh! Clippety-clop. Shhhh! Clippety-clop. Shhhhh! They had to be VERY quiet until they were out of the city.

Then on and ON they went. For days and days and DAYS. FINALLY—they were SAFE in the land of Egypt! There they stayed while baby Jesus grew and grew. Then, one night—

God sent an angel to Joseph AGAIN. "The wicked king is dead," the angel said. "You can take Mary and Jesus back home now." And that's JUST what Joseph did! Back they went on the long LONG trip day after day. Finally, they were safe at home again.

All that time, Jesus was growing and growing taller and stronger. And all that time God was helping Mary and Joseph take care of Him. Yes, every minute!   MATTHEW 2:13-23

Mary and Joseph and baby Jesus were a happy family. How did God help Mary and Joseph take care of baby Jesus?

Can you name some ways your family takes care of you? Because God always loves you and gives you a family to care for you and protect you, thank Him for His loving care.

Thank You, dear God, for loving me and being kind and good. Thank You for my family and for the loving care they give me.   Amen.

WHEN JESUS WAS A LITTLE CHILD

When Jesus was a little child—
A little child like me—
He ran and played,
He worked and helped;
He loved His family.

A busy, happy child He was!
And as He grew, He learned
The Bible words
And stories, too.
The same ones I have heard!

I'm glad that Jesus, God's
    Son, grew
And was a child like me!
Sometimes He felt
The way I feel—
SO tired! But SO happy.

For then, when work and play
    was done,
He climbed on Mary's knee.
And lovingly
She rocked her boy
'Til fast asleep He'd be.

The little boy Jesus grew and lived with His family in Nazareth. What do you think He did that you do?

Mary and Joseph and little Jesus talked about God and prayed to Him. Our family can read together about God and talk to God, too. How does talking to God help us?

Dear God, we are glad for Your Word. Help us to love to read the Bible and to talk to You. Thank You for our family.   Amen.

GROWING
AS GOD PLANNED

STORY 50

Were you ever a little baby? Are you a little baby now? You grew and grew, bigger and bigger, didn't you? The Bible tells us that Jesus was not always a little baby. But Jesus grew and grew just like you are growing.

Jesus learned to walk, just like you did. Jesus learned to talk. He learned to work and play, too. Yes, Jesus grew bigger and stronger, like you are growing.

When Jesus was still a little boy, His family went to live in Nazareth. At one side of their house in Nazareth was a carpenter's shop. Joseph worked there to make tables and chairs, doors and all kinds of things for the people to buy. Jesus watched Joseph making things out of wood. He learned how to help and make things like Joseph did in the carpenter's shop.

Mary and Joseph showed Jesus how to work and be a good helper. They also taught Him to be obedient. They told Him that God's Word said children should be obedient. This was part of growing as God planned.

Jesus learned more and more as He grew bigger and bigger. Jesus had birthdays. . . three. . . four. . . five. . . six. . . seven. . . eight. . . just as you do. He learned to do what He was asked to do. Jesus obeyed Mary and Joseph "in all things" because He loved the Lord God.

102   LUKE 2:30-40

God's book, the Bible, says, *Children, obey your parents in all things* (Colossians 3:20). Did little Jesus obey Mary and Joseph? Do you obey your parents? How did you obey them today?

God wants boys and girls to obey their parents *in all things,* as Jesus did. Sometimes, is it hard to obey? Who will help you to obey? Right now you can bow your head and ask the Lord to help you obey *in all things.*

LIVING IN NAZARETH

Jesus was a busy, HAPPY child living with Mary and Joseph. And day after day the little Lord Jesus grew and GREW! Taller and stronger, just as you are growing!

Right beside Jesus' house in Nazareth was Joseph's workshop. While Jesus was a little boy, He watched Joseph in the workshop make tables and chairs and doors and—just all KINDS of things!

What fun it was to see the wood shavings and bits of sawdust falling to the floor as Joseph sawed and planed the wood. Then, when the floor had to be swept, Jesus was a glad helper— even when He was a LITTLE boy.

When He grew bigger and stronger, Jesus sawed the wood—scchhhscchh! He cut and planed each piece until it was smooth and straight, and JUST the right size.

When Jesus was just a little older than you are, He went to school. There He learned to read and write. And when His work was done JUST RIGHT, He ran to play with other boys. What fun they must have had!

And then—there were quiet times every day when Jesus' family talked to God. And there were times when Mary and Joseph told Him stories from God's Word. Some of the very same Bible stories YOU like to hear!

So—day after day, day after day, Jesus grew taller and stronger. What a busy, happy child He was! For He LOVED the Lord God, His Father in heaven.

104 LUKE 2:39, 40

How much have you grown this year? What are some things you can do now that you could not do last year?

Jesus grew just as you are growing. He was a glad helper in His home. What did He do to help Joseph in the workshop? He always did His best at home and school.

What things do you do to show that you are a glad helper at home, at school, and at church? Do you always do your very best?

THE BOY JESUS IN
THE TEMPLE-CHURCH

Jesus grew and grew. He learned to talk. He learned to walk. He learned to work and play. When Jesus was a big boy, twelve years old, Mary and Joseph said to Him, "You are old enough to go with us on the long trip to the temple-church in Jerusalem."

How happy Jesus was to help Mary and Joseph get ready for the trip. At last everything was ready. Down the long road Jesus walked with Mary and Joseph. Along the way they met friends going to the temple-church, too.

When Jesus and His family came near Jerusalem, they saw the shining roof of the beautiful temple-church high up on the hill. Up, up, up they walked until they reached the steps of the temple-church. Then they went through the big gates to the lovely house of God.

In the temple-church Jesus listened. He heard the choir sing Bible songs He knew. He heard the minister pray. Jesus prayed, too.

Jesus found a place in the temple-church where some teachers were talking about the Lord God. He listened and He talked with them. What a good time Jesus had talking about the Lord God in the temple-church!

After a while Mary and Joseph came to tell Jesus it was time to leave the temple-church. As they walked on the long trip home, Jesus told Mary and Joseph about the wonderful time He had in the temple-church. Jesus knew that God was pleased when His people came to worship and hear His Word at their temple-church. LUKE 2:40-52

106

How happy Jesus was to be old enough to go to the temple-church! He was glad to go with Mary and Joseph. What did Jesus do in the temple-church? Tell three things you especially like to do in our church.

The Bible says, *I was glad when they said . . . , Let us go into the house of the Lord* (Psalm 122:1). Let us thank God for our church.

GOD'S MESSENGER

John the Baptist was God's special messenger. He did not live in a city or a town. He lived in the desert all by himself. His food was sweet wild honey that the bees made. His clothes were made of camel skins.

While he lived in the desert, John the Baptist learned what the special work was that God had for him to do. "Tell the people Jesus is My Son," God said. "Tell them Jesus is the promised Saviour."

So John the Baptist left the desert and went to a place near the river. There, he told the people the important news, "A wonderful man is coming. This man is God's Son."

People came from the cities and the towns to hear John the Baptist. "God kept His promise to you. He has sent you the Saviour Who is God's own Son." The people listened to the important news about Jesus.

One day while John the Baptist was talking to the people near the river, Jesus Himself came and stood nearby. While Jesus was there, John the Baptist heard God speak from heaven. "This is My Son Whom I love," God said. "I am well pleased with Him."

John the Baptist was a good messenger. He told many people of Jesus. He wanted them to know that God sent His Son Jesus to be the promised Saviour.

You can be a good messenger, too. You can tell all your friends about God's Son, the Lord **108** Jesus. LUKE 3:16-23; JOHN 1:29-34

Did you ever deliver a message to someone for Mother? Father? Teacher? A messenger has a very special and important job to do.

John the Baptist was God's special messenger. What special work did God ask John the Baptist to do? What important news did he tell the people?

Think of one of your friends who does not know that Jesus is God's Son. You can be a good messenger! You can tell him about Jesus.

JESUS IN THE SYNAGOGUE-CHURCH

When Jesus was a grown-up man, He went one day to the little town of Nazareth. There He went to worship with His friends at the synagogue-church. When it was time to unroll the big Bible scroll, the minister asked Jesus to read God's Word to the people.

From the Bible scroll Jesus read God's wonderful promise to send a Saviour. "The Saviour will show how much I love you," God's Word said. Jesus finished reading from God's Word. Then He said to the people, "I am the One God has sent to be your Saviour."

On another day Jesus and His friends traveled to the temple-church in Jerusalem. When they came near the temple they heard loud noises. Men were selling love gifts for the people to give in the temple-church. Instead of being beautiful and quiet, the temple-church was a noisy place.

Jesus knew this was not right. So He spoke in a loud voice to the men. "Take these animals away." Jesus said, "This is not a place to buy and sell. This is a place to worship. This is the house of God!" Quickly they took the animals out of the courtyard. The temple-church was a quiet place again.

Then Jesus and His friends went into the beautiful temple-church. They heard lovely music and singing. They listened to the minister read God's Word. They prayed to God. Because they loved the Lord God, they worshiped in the temple-church.

110   LUKE 4:14-32; 19:45-48

These men and boys were listening quietly and carefully to the reading of the Bible scroll. They wanted to hear God's Word. One time Jesus saw some people in the temple-church doing something that displeased Him. What did Jesus tell them?

How does God want you to act in our church? What things should you do and not do in church? The Bible tells us, *thou* (you) *oughtest* (ought) *to behave thyself* (yourself) *in the house of God* (I Timothy 3:15).

111

CHOOSING
SPECIAL HELPERS

One day when Jesus was a grown-up man, He was walking by the lake. There He stopped to watch two of His friends who were fishermen. They were throwing their fishing nets out into the water to catch fish.

"Simon! Andrew!" Jesus called to them. "Come! Be My helpers!" Right THEN—Simon and Andrew hurried to put away their nets and go with Jesus. Now Jesus had TWO helpers. But they were not all.

As Jesus and His two helpers walked along, they saw two other fishermen. THEIR names were James and John. And they were helping their father fix the fishing nets. "James!" "John!" Jesus called to them. "Come! Be My helpers!" And right THEN—James and John hurried to put away their nets and GO with Jesus. So now Jesus had FOUR helpers—Simon, Andrew, James and John. But they were not all.

On other days Jesus asked more and MORE men to be His helpers. Finally, He had TWELVE! These twelve helpers heard the Lord Jesus tell them of God, His Heavenly Father. And day after day they learned WONDERFUL things about the Lord Jesus, too!

What do you think was the MOST wonderful thing they learned? That God LOVED them. And sent the Lord Jesus to show how MUCH He LOVED them!

Jesus' helpers were glad to learn more and more about Him. For they loved Jesus and wanted to be GOOD helpers. MATTHEW 4:18-22

112

Jesus chose special helpers to learn of Him. Can you name four of the men Jesus asked to be His helpers? Jesus said, *Come . . . learn of me* (Matthew 11:28, 29). How can we come and learn more about Jesus today?

Dear God, thank You for giving us the Bible to help us learn of You. Thank You for parents and special helpers in our church who help us learn about You. In Jesus' name.   Amen.   **113**

OUR LOVING LORD

What a happy day this was! "We're Go–ing to see JE–sus!" The children's singing voices were a happy sound as the mothers and fathers and boys and girls walked along the road.

"My mother says I can go and TALK to Jesus!" one happy child said.

"And my mother said that I could even go close enough to TOUCH Him!" another little child said.

"Come on!" one of the children called. "Let's pick these flowers and give them to Jesus." And so they skipped–and–ran–and skipped–and–ran on their way to see JESUS.

But when they came near—Ohh! They could not see Him through the crowd. Some mothers and fathers tried to make a way for their children in–and–out–and–around the many people.

When they were almost to Jesus—

"Stand back!" some of Jesus' helpers said. "You are in the way. Jesus is TOO busy to bother with children now!"

But wait! JESUS was speaking to His helpers. "ALWAYS let the children come to Me! I WANT to see them!"

Right away the helpers let the children run to Jesus. Some gave Him flowers. And some even climbed up on His lap. Jesus put His arms around them and blessed them all.

What a happy day! The children knew Jesus LOVED them! And the grownups knew the Lord God in heaven loves little children in a **114** very special way! MATTHEW 18:3-7; 19:13-15

What would you do if you knew that the Lord Jesus was coming to our city? What did the children do long ago? How did the children know that Jesus loved them? What do you think they did to show their love for Jesus?

Jesus loves you. What can you do to show your love for Him? Do all your friends know that Jesus loves them? You can tell them the Bible story about the children who went to see Jesus.

A NEW PRAYER

Now it was nighttime. Jesus had been helping the people all day. "Please come and stay at my house tonight," said Peter, one of Jesus' helpers. So Jesus stayed at Peter's house.

When morning came, the sound of voices outside awoke Peter and the other helpers. They looked out and saw many, many people. The people had come back to see Jesus.

Peter went to Jesus' room, but Jesus was not there. His helpers looked everywhere in the house, but Jesus was not there. Peter said to the others, "Let us go to find Jesus."

Down the road Peter and the other helpers went looking for Jesus. In a quiet place on the hillside they found the Lord Jesus. He was praying. He was talking to God, His Heavenly Father.

When Jesus had finished talking to God, the helpers asked, "Will you teach us to pray?"

"When you pray," Jesus said, "you are talking to God Who always loves you. God knows all about you. God always hears you and will help you." Then Jesus taught His helpers this prayer.

"Our Father which art in heaven,
Hallowed be thy name.
Thy kingdom come.
Thy will be done in earth, as it is in heaven.
Give us this day our daily bread.
And forgive us our debts, as we forgive our debtors.
And lead us not into temptation, but deliver us from evil:
For thine is the kingdom, and the power, and the glory,
for ever. Amen."

MATTHEW 6:5-13; MARK 1:35-37

When Jesus finished praying, what did His helpers ask Him? Jesus helped His friends learn to pray. The prayer He taught them is in the Bible. Let's read it together (Matthew 6:9-13). What did Jesus talk to God about? (Giving food, forgiving each other, doing what is right.)

Aren't we glad to know that God hears His children pray? No matter where we are when we talk to God, *we know that he hear*(s) *us* (I John 5:15).

A THANKFUL FRIEND

One day Jesus went to the church and taught the people many wonderful things from the Word of God. Peter and some of Jesus' other helpers were there, too.

When church was over, Peter invited Jesus and the helpers to his house. There they could rest. And they could all have supper together. Jesus and His helpers were glad to go with Peter. But when they came to Peter's house—

They found that the grandmother was SICK! She had a fever that made her feel VERY sick. And right away they asked Jesus to help her. And THIS is what He did.

He went to the room where the grandmother was. He stood there by her bed. And He took her hand. Gently, He helped her UP. First, she SAT up. Then, she STOOD up. And then— she WALKED! The fever was gone! She felt fine! Yes, the Lord Jesus made her well!

Oh how glad she was to be well again! She was so glad that she wanted to do something for the Lord Jesus right away. So she went to the kitchen. She fixed some food. Set the table. And then she served Jesus and His helpers the good supper she had made for them. Wasn't that a lovely way to show her LOVE and THANKS to Jesus for making her well!

The Lord Jesus and His helpers must have been glad for a time to rest and to have supper together at Peter's house. And EVERYONE was happy because the Lord Jesus made the grandmother well!   MARK 1:21, 22, 29-31

How did Jesus help at Peter's house? Why do you think Jesus made the grandmother well? How did the grandmother show her love and thanks to the Lord Jesus?

The Lord Jesus always loves and helps our family. How can you thank Him for this loving care? Being kind and helping others are ways to show your love. What can you do to help your friends and your family?

BRINGING
A FRIEND TO JESUS

STORY 59

The sick man just lay on his mat. He was too sick even to stand up. BUT, this sick man had kind FRIENDS.

And one day these friends heard the best news—that JESUS was in town! "If only our sick friend could see Jesus!" they thought. "JESUS could make him well!"

"If only I COULD see Jesus!" the sick man said. "But HOW could I get to the place where Jesus is?"

"Don't worry about THAT!" the kind friends said. "We will CARRY you!" And they DID! Each friend held a corner of the sick man's mat. And carefully they carried him. When they came to the house where Jesus was—why, there was such a crowd that they could not even get NEAR!

Then they had an IDEA! And up-Up-UP the stairs to the flat roof of the house they carried the sick man. Quickly they worked until—

They made a HOLE in the roof! Tightly they held the ropes at the corners of the mat. Then, down-Down-DOWN they lowered the sick man until he was inside the house. And right in front of JESUS! Looking at the sick man, Jesus said to him, "Pick up your mat and WALK."

WALK! That's just what Jesus said! And that's exactly what the man did! THIS man had been too sick to walk, even a little bit. Now he was WELL!

Just think how HAPPY he was! But especially, how HAPPY his kind friends were that they had brought him to the Lord Jesus!   MARK 2:1-12

What did the sick man's friends say Jesus could do for him? What did the friends do?

Jesus said to the sick man, "Your sins are forgiven." What else did Jesus say to him? When the people saw the man get up and walk, they were so happy that they glorified God (praised Him).

Does Jesus forgive our sins? Make us well? How can we praise Him?

A CALL FOR HELP

In Bible times there was a very important soldier. He had many helpers, and they all did the work he asked them to do. BUT—one of the soldier's best helpers was VERY sick. He was much too sick to work for the soldier.

Someone told the soldier about the ways Jesus helped the people. The soldier decided to ask Jesus to make his helper well. So the soldier asked some friends to find Jesus.

When the soldier's friends found Jesus, they said, "Please, come with us to help our soldier friend. Come and make his good helper well." The Lord Jesus was always glad to help others. So off He went with the friends, toward the soldier's house.

Before they came to the house, the soldier sent other friends to Jesus. And they said, "Our soldier friend doesn't want you to BOTHER coming all the way to his house, Jesus. Just SAY that his helper will be well. And the soldier knows his good helper will then be well."

Jesus looked at the people standing around Him. "Isn't this AMAZING!" He said. "This soldier believes I can make his helper well just by SAYING 'be well!' I have not met anyone who believes in Me like this soldier does!"

And do you know what happened? When the friends went back to the soldier's house, the helper was perfectly well! The soldier must have been so very glad! What a wonderful thing Jesus did—all because He LOVED the soldier and was glad to help him.

122 LUKE 7:1-10

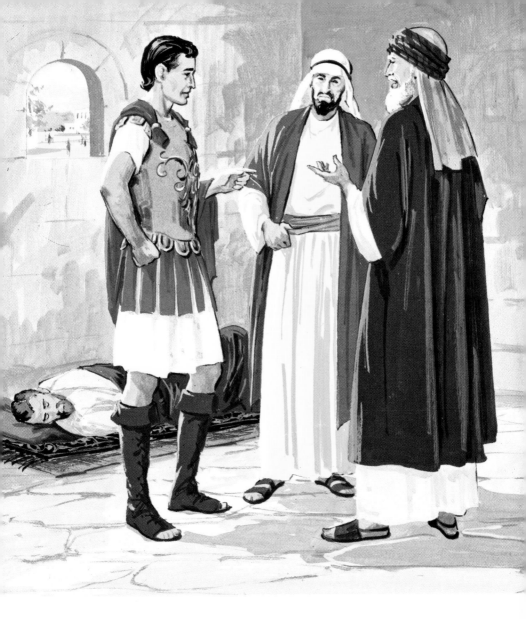

Find the soldier in the picture. One of his best helpers is lying down. What is the matter with him? What is the soldier asking his friends to do?

Did Jesus go to the soldier's home? What did Jesus do to help the soldier? Tell the story in your own words.

Jesus is pleased when we believe Him and what He tells us in the Bible.

STORY 61 WINDS OBEY

One day, by the beautiful blue lake, Jesus was teaching the people about God. By nighttime Jesus was VERY tired. He said to His helpers, "Let us go across to the other side of the lake."

So they said good-by to the people and got into a little boat. While the helpers rowed and rowed Jesus lay down on a pillow at the back of the boat. And there He went to SLEEP.

Everything was quiet! The tiny waves went slap-slap against the boat. The moon and the stars shone in the nighttime sky. Then—very suddenly—

Wooaoo!—went the wind. And it turned the tiny waves into GREAT BIG WAVES. Whissh! —went the waves, splashing more and more water into the boat. Black, dark clouds blew across the sky and covered the moon and the stars. The helpers were AFRAID!

"Lord Jesus!" the helpers called out. "Our boat is sinking!"

Right away, Jesus woke up. He felt the strong wind blowing. And He saw the big waves splashing water into the boat. Then—He SPOKE to the strong wind and the big waves, "Hush! Be still!" The strong wind stopped blowing! The big waves stopped splashing! The Lord Jesus, God's Son, had made everything quiet again.

"Why were you afraid?" Jesus asked. "Didn't you KNOW I would take care of you?"

Now the helpers KNEW that they did not need to be afraid. For the Lord Jesus would ALWAYS be their helper.

124 MARK 4:35-41

Jesus helped the men in the boat. How did He help them? Why did He say they should not be afraid?

Are you afraid sometimes? (Let your child tell of times he has been afraid.) You can remember this Bible verse, *The Lord is my helper* (Hebrews 13:6). The Lord Jesus will always help you and take care of you because He loves you. Aren't you glad!

A CHILD MADE WELL

In Bible times there was a father named Jairus. But Jairus was a sad father for his little girl was very sick. Jairus did all he could to help her get well. Her mother did all she could. But still the child was very sick. "I will find JESUS," Jairus decided. "He will help my little girl!"

So Jairus hurried down the road to the side of the beautiful blue lake where Jesus was. Jairus squeezed his way through the crowds of people until—he FOUND Jesus.

"Oh Jesus, my little girl is SO sick," Jairus said, "PLEASE, come and make her well!" Right away Jesus called three of His helpers and was ready to go with Jairus. And then—a man came hurrying from Jairus' house!

"It's too late! Don't ask Jesus to come with you now," the man said to Jairus. "Your child is dead!"

But Jesus said, "Don't be afraid, Jairus. Just believe that I will help your little girl." So Jesus and his three helpers went right on with Jairus all the way to his house. Up to the door and into the house Jesus went with Jairus. Then, into the little girl's room and right up to her bed! Jesus took her hand and gently said, "Little girl, get UP now."

First, the little girl opened her eyes. She sat up. Then she got up from her bed. She was WELL! Jairus was SO happy! The mother was SO happy! And SO was the little girl! All because the Lord Jesus loved them and helped them!

MARK 5:22,23,35-42

How happy Jairus and his family felt! They wanted to thank the Lord Jesus for His help. Find the person in the picture that Jesus helped. Why do you think Jesus helped the little girl?

Only Jesus could make the little girl come alive because Jesus is God's Son.

Dear God, we are glad Jesus loved the little girl and made her alive. We are glad Jesus loves and helps us, too. In Jesus' name. Amen.

127

DEAF EARS
MADE TO HEAR

In Bible times there was a man who could SEE everything. But he could not HEAR. He could not hear the songs of birds, or the pitter-patter of rain. And he could not hear what people said! There was SO much he did not KNOW.

And he did not ASK many questions! For he could not TALK just right. There was SO much he could only wonder about. Until—

"Jesus is coming!" the people were saying. "He is coming this way!"

This man could not hear what the people said. But his friends heard, and took him to the place where Jesus was! "Oh, Jesus!" the friends said, "help this man. Put your hands on him so he can hear. So he can talk just right, too." And do you know what happened then?

First, Jesus took the man to a more quiet place —away from all the people. Jesus touched the man's ears. He touched the man's tongue. And then Jesus looked up to heaven and spoke. Suddenly—

The man could HEAR! People's voices—birds' songs—wind blowing—EVERYTHING! And he could talk just right, too! There was SO much he wanted to know. NOW he could find out! And do you know what? The best thing he found out was that Jesus was the One Who loved him and helped him.

Oh, how glad he was that he could hear Jesus' voice. And that he could say thank-You to Jesus!

128   MARK 7:32-37

What was the first sound you heard when you woke up today? Did you hear a bird singing? Or did you hear Mother calling you to breakfast? Aren't you glad for ears that hear and a voice that can speak!

You can use your voice to sing to God and to say thank you for His love and care. The Bible says, *It is a good thing to give thanks unto the Lord, and to sing praises* (Psalm 92:1). **129**

A MAN WHO WANTED TO SEE

In Bible times there was a man named Bartimaeus who could not see ANYTHING. No trees. No flowers. No children. No people—not even his own father or mother! He was BLIND!

All he did every day was sit by the side of the road and wait for people to give him money to buy food. So Bartimaeus waited and LISTENED. Then ONE day—

Bartimaeus heard many people coming down the road. Someone said that with all those people were Jesus and His helpers. Now Bartimaeus knew that Jesus loved and helped people. "I think I will ASK Jesus to help me!" Bartimaeus thought. And that's just what Bartimaeus DID! "Jesus! help me!" Bartimaeus called out. People nearby told him to be quiet. But Bartimaeus kept calling out—"Jesus! Jesus, HELP me!" And then—

Bartimaeus heard someone say to him, "Be quiet and get up now. Jesus is calling you!" Right away, Bartimaeus jumped up. And someone helped him to hurry to Jesus.

"What do you want me to do for you?" Jesus asked him.

"Lord Jesus," said Bartimaeus, "I want to SEE!" And right away, Bartimaeus could see! He could see trees and flowers! He could see children and people!

Now Bartimaeus could do more than just LISTEN. For Jesus loved him and helped him to SEE! And BEST of all, Bartimaeus could SEE the Lord Jesus!

130　　MARK 10:46-52

Close your eyes and feel the picture. Can you tell by feeling the picture how many people are in it? Can you name the colors of their clothes? God gave us eyes to see colors and all the wonderful things He has made. Our eyes help us to see how we can help people, too.

Thank You, dear God, for eyes that see. Help us to use our eyes to see ways we can help others. In Jesus' name. Amen.

BRINGING LOVE GIFTS
TO THE TEMPLE-CHURCH

Many people came to bring their love gifts to the temple-church. Jesus and His friends were there, too. They watched the people placing their gifts in the offering boxes.

Many rich people came by dressed in beautiful clothes. They felt very very important. They wanted everyone to see how much money they gave. These rich people dropped many big pieces of money into the offering box. Although these rich people gave much money, they also kept much for themselves.

Then there came a very poor woman. Her clothes were not beautiful. Quietly she waited while the rich people went by. Perhaps she was thinking, "I hope no one sees me give these two little pieces of money. I wish I had more. But I am glad to give all I have."

Slowly the poor woman walked to the offering box. Clink, clink, went her two little pieces of money as they dropped into the box.

Jesus saw the woman. He loved her and knew all about her. Jesus knew how poor she was. He knew how much she loved the Lord. He knew she gave all she had.

Then Jesus said to His friends, "This poor woman gave more than all the rich people."

"But she gave only two small pieces of money," His friends said.

"Yes," said Jesus. "The rich people kept much money for themselves. But the poor woman gave all she had!" Jesus was glad that she loved the Lord God so much.

132   MARK 12:41-44

How do you feel when you receive a gift? When someone gives you a gift he is happy when you like the gift.

Why was Jesus pleased when the woman brought her love gift to the temple-church? What love gift can you give to show you love the Lord Jesus? Is God pleased when you are not a glad, cheerful giver? The Bible says, *God loveth* (loves) *a cheerful giver* (II Corinthians 9:7).

A KIND HELPER

One day Jesus told the people this story. There was a man who started on a trip. And as he walked along, some robbers came and took away all his MONEY. They tore his clothes and hurt him. Then they ran away.

The poor man was hurt all over. He was too hurt even to walk. And he was very thirsty lying there in the hot sun. Soon, step-step-step—

Someone was coming down the road! "Oh, maybe it's someone who will help me!" the hurt man thought. Closer the traveler came. He saw the hurt man. But walked on by! Ohhh!

The sun got hotter. The hurt man got thirstier. Then, step-step-step—

Someone was coming down the road! "Oh surely, this one will help me!" the hurt man thought. Closer this traveler came. He saw the hurt man. And HE walked right on by! Ohhhhh!

The sun got HOTTER. The poor man got THIRSTIER. And the sore places HURT so very much! Then, clippety-clop, clippety-clop—

Along came a man riding a donkey. "Oh, surely THIS traveler will stop!" the hurt man thought. This traveler saw the hurt man. He STOPPED! Climbed off his donkey. And went to help the poor hurt man.

First, he gave the hurt man a drink. Put medicine and bandages on the sore places. Then he lifted the hurt man up on the donkey. Took him to a hotel. And there he cared for him! Before the traveler left he paid the hotelkeeper

134 to care for the hurt man! LUKE 10:30-37

After Jesus told this story He asked a question. He said, "Who is my neighbor?" Can you answer His question? Which person in the story was the kind of helper the Lord Jesus wants you to be?

Think of ways you can be a good neighbor and helper today. (Share toys or books with a friend, take flowers or cookies to a neighbor, send card to a sick friend, etc.)

STORY 67 LOVING FRIENDS

One day Jesus went to visit two of His friends. One was Mary. The other was her sister Martha. Mary and Martha were so GLAD that JESUS came to see them!

When Jesus came, Mary thought to herself, "Oh, I'm so GLAD Jesus is here! Now I can talk with Him. And BEST of all, I can LISTEN to what He says."

So Mary just sat right down beside Jesus so she could hear EVERY word He said. She was happy as can be LISTENING to Him. For Mary LOVED the Lord Jesus!

And when Martha saw Him, she thought to herself, "Oh, I'm so GLAD Jesus is here! He must be tired and hungry after His long walk to our house. I will make a good dinner for Him!"

So Martha hurried to get fruits and vegetables and meat ready. She m–i–x–e–d and st–i–rr–ed flour and oil to make little cakes. Oh, she was busy as can be making a good dinner for Him. For Martha LOVED the Lord Jesus.

Mary listened and LISTENED while the Lord Jesus told her how VERY much God loved her.

And all the time Mary was listening to Jesus, Martha was making a DELICIOUS dinner for Him. She got out her best dishes. And she set the table. Then—it was time for dinner!

How GLAD the Lord Jesus was that Martha made the delicious dinner because she LOVED Him. And He was VERY glad that Mary WANTED to talk with Him, and LISTEN to

136 Him—because she LOVED Him. LUKE 10:38-42

Mary and Martha were good friends of the Lord Jesus. They were glad when He visited them. What did Martha do to show her love for the Lord Jesus? How did Mary show her love?

How can you show your love for the Lord Jesus? One way you can show your love is by reading the Bible and listening to Bible stories that tell about Him.

137

A GOOD SHEPHERD

One day Jesus told the people this story. There was a shepherd who had one hundred sheep. This shepherd knew the name of each one of his sheep. And they all knew their shepherd's voice.

In the morning this shepherd let his sheep out on the hillsides. There the sheep ate the green grass they wanted. And they drank the quiet, cool water in the little stream at the bottom of the hill.

Sometimes the shepherd kept his sheep in a place called a fold. This fold was a big yard with a stone wall around it. At night the shepherd slept right across the DOORWAY of the fold. "No one can get into the fold and hurt MY sheep!" he said. He took care of them every MINUTE. He was a GOOD shepherd.

One day the shepherd was counting his sheep. But OH MY! One sheep was GONE!

Right away the shepherd went out to find his lost sheep. He looked and LOOKED. He called and CALLED the sheep's name. Then—

"Baaaaa!" What was that? Again he heard, "BAAAA!" And THERE was the lost sheep— with his soft woolly coat caught in the bushes. The shepherd had FOUND his sheep! And all the way home he carried the sheep.

Then the good shepherd called to his friends, "Come and be glad with me! For I have found my sheep!" And best of all, the sheep was back with the kind shepherd who always loved and cared for him.   LUKE 15:3-7; JOHN 10:1-16

The shepherd loved each one of his sheep. How did he take care of them during the day? How did he care for them at night? He was a very good shepherd.

The Bible says, *The Lord is my shepherd* (Psalm 23:1). (Help your child learn Psalm 23.) The Lord Jesus loves and cares for you just like the shepherd loves and cares for his sheep.

Thank You, Lord Jesus, for loving me and taking care of me. I am glad that you are my Good Shepherd. In Jesus' name.   Amen.   **139**

A LOVING FATHER

One day Jesus told the people this story. There was a father who had two boys. This father had fine clothes, plenty of good food and a beautiful home for his boys.

When these two boys grew up, one of them said to his father one day, "I would like to have all the money now that you promised me." And the father gave it to him.

Soon, the boy took his money and went to live in another country. There, he did many wrong things. And he spent his money on many things that were NOT good. Soon, all his money was GONE. Every bit of it!

The boy had no money to buy food. And he was hungry! He began to think about his beautiful home. But most of all he thought about his loving father. Then, the boy decided, "I'll go home and tell my father I'm SORRY for the many wrong things I have done." So he did.

When he was almost home, his father came running to meet him! The father was so VERY glad to see his boy again! "Oh, father," said the boy, "I've done so MANY wrong things! But I am VERY sorry!"

The father could tell that his boy was REALLY sorry. Of course, the father was glad to make everything all right again. For he ALWAYS loved his boy.

The father gave his boy new clothes. And new shoes! He even had special food cooked. And he invited friends to a wonderful PARTY

for his boy who came home.   LUKE 15:11-24

The picture shows how happy the father was to have his son home. What part of the story does it tell?

Jesus told this story because He wanted the people to know that God loves His children even when they sin—do wrong things. When we are really sorry for what we have done and are willing to stop doing it, God will forgive us just as the father forgave his son.

The Bible says, *If we confess our sins, he* (God) *. . . will forgive us* (I John 1:9).

TEN GLAD MEN

In Bible times there were ten sick men. ALL of them. They were so sick that they could not even live with their families and friends. No one wanted to be near these ten sick men and become sick like they were. So day after day these sick men lived outside the city. And they were very sad. All of them. Then, ONE day—

"Jesus is coming!" they heard people saying. "He's coming to our city!"

When the sick men heard this, they thought, "Ooh, maybe Jesus will make us WELL!" And they hurried to wait by the road for Jesus.

Sure enough, along came Jesus. Closer and closer. The ten sick men began to call out. "Jesus—HELP us! Jesus—HELP us!" And Jesus heard ALL of them! He stopped. He looked with love at these ten sick men. ALL of them!

Then Jesus said "Go now to your church and show your minister you are all well." And sure enough, they WERE! The sickness was gone from ALL of them. They were SO happy! Down the road they ran as fast as they could go toward the city. But then—

ONE of them stopped. He came running back to Jesus. "Oh THANK You, Jesus, for making me well," he said.

"I made ALL of you well," Jesus said. "Where are the other men?" They had GONE! They forgot to say "THANK You, Jesus!"

But the man who came back—Oh, how he
142 LOVED Jesus for helping him! LUKE 17:11-19

How many men did Jesus help? How many came back to thank Jesus? Jesus was happy to hear the man say thank you.

Our parents are glad when we say thank you for the way they love us and care for us. Jesus is happy, too, when we say thank you for His love and care.

We thank You now, dear God in heaven, for food and home today. We thank You for Your love and care. In Jesus' name we pray.   Amen.   **143**

A FORGIVEN FRIEND

In Bible times there was a very RICH man named Zacchaeus. But Zacchaeus was not HAPPY. For he did what he KNEW was wrong. He took money that did not belong to him!

One day, Jesus came to the town where Zacchaeus lived. "I am going to see what kind of a person Jesus is," Zacchaeus decided. And off he hurried to the road where Jesus was walking with His helpers. But when he got there—

He couldn't SEE Jesus! For Zacchaeus was a little man. And even on tiptoe he was not tall enough to look over the heads of the people waiting to see Jesus. But then—Zacchaeus had an idea. He ran to a big TREE. And he climbed up–Up–UP the tree. Now he could see over ALL the people! Zacchaeus waited. And watched and watched.

Finally, he could see Jesus coming. Closer and CLOSER—until right UNDER that tree the Lord Jesus STOPPED! He looked right UP at Zacchaeus. And right away Zacchaeus knew that Jesus loved him.

"Come down, Zacchaeus," said Jesus. "I want to visit at your house today." And Zacchaeus climbed down–Down–DOWN from that tree.

"How wonderful!" Zacchaeus thought. "Jesus LOVES ME!" And right away Zacchaeus loved the Lord Jesus. Zacchaeus was SORRY now for the wrong things he had done! He wanted to give BACK all the money he had taken. And give money to the POOR people, too! For Zacchaeus **144** LOVED the Lord Jesus.   LUKE 19:1-9

Zacchaeus wanted to see Jesus. What did he do? How did Zacchaeus feel when Jesus spoke to him? Was Zacchaeus sorry for the wrong things he had done? Then what did Zacchaeus want to do? Jesus loved Zacchaeus and forgave him.

Jesus loves you, too. He is glad to forgive your sins if you are really sorry. Tell God right now that you are sorry for your sins and ask Him to forgive you. He will forgive you. (See I John 1:9.)

THE HELPFUL GUEST

Have you ever gone to a wedding party? Jesus went to a wedding party one day . . . His mother was there, too.

The people were talking together and eating at the wedding party. Soon there was not enough wine. So many people had come to the wedding party that all the wine was gone.

Jesus' mother heard that there was not enough wine. "The party is not over yet, but the wine is gone!" she told Jesus. She knew that Jesus could help.

Standing by the wall were six big jars. Jesus saw the jars and said to the servants, "Fill all those jars with water."

The servants did not know that it was Jesus, God's Son, Who spoke to them. But they did as He told them. They filled one jar, two jars, three, four, five, six big jars full of water. Right up to the top.

Then the Lord Jesus said to the servants, "Take some to the man who is giving this party." When the servants dipped into the jars, the jars were full of wine! A wonderful thing had happened! Jesus had changed the water into wine!

When the man tasted the wine the servants brought, it was so good that he said, "Everyone usually serves the good wine first but the best wine has been saved until now." He did not know that Jesus had changed the water in the jars into wine. He did not know that the Lord Jesus, God's own Son, was the helpful Guest Who had done this wonderful thing.

146   JOHN 2:1-11

One day Jesus helped at a wedding party. What did He do? Why do you think He helped?

Jesus helps people in many ways. Because Jesus is God's Son, He can help by doing things you and I cannot do.

We want to be good helpers because we love Jesus. How can you be a helper at home today? The Bible tells us, (We) *are helpers* (II Corinthians 1:24).

A NIGHTTIME VISITOR

In the big city of Jerusalem there lived a man named Nicodemus.

Nicodemus knew many things about God. He had heard Jesus tell the people about God. But Nicodemus wanted to know more. He decided to go and talk to Jesus.

One night Nicodemus went to the house where Jesus stayed. Jesus was very glad Nicodemus had come. Jesus knew that Nicodemus had come to hear more about God.

"Teacher," Nicodemus said to Jesus, "We know God has sent You. No one else could do all the wonderful things You do."

"Yes, God has sent Me," Jesus said to Nicodemus. "God loves everyone so much that He wants them to be His children. I have come so everyone may belong to God's family and live in heaven with Him some day."

"How can this wonderful thing be," Nicodemus asked. "How can I belong to God's family?"

"You may belong to God's family when you believe I am God's Son, the Saviour," Jesus said.

Nicodemus listened. He thought about all that Jesus was saying. "I am God's only Son," Jesus said. "God sent Me into the world. He sent Me to be the Saviour. All who believe I am their Saviour have everlasting life and a home in heaven for ever and ever."

Nicodemus and Jesus talked a long time. Nicodemus thought and thought about these wonderful things Jesus had told him. He was glad he **148** had talked with Jesus.   JOHN 3:1-18; 7:50,51

Jesus told Nicodemus something that is important for us to know, too. It was how to belong to God's family. Do you remember what He said? (If child does not recall what Jesus said, reread story.)

God loves everybody in the world and wants each one to be with Him in heaven someday. God sent Jesus to tell everyone that He loves them and that He wants them to be His children. Isn't that wonderful? Do you belong to God's family?

THE FORGOTTEN JAR

Jesus and His helpers walked and walked along the dusty road until they came to a cool place by a well. Jesus stayed by the well while His helpers went to buy food.

While Jesus was resting, a woman came to the well. She came to get water in the big jar she carried. "Will you please give me a drink of water?" Jesus asked her.

The woman was surprised to have this man speak to her. She did not know Who Jesus was. But she listened while Jesus talked to her about God. Then she asked Jesus a question: "Do we have to go to a special place when we sing and pray to God?"

"There is no special place to worship God," Jesus answered, "God hears His people wherever they are."

The woman still wondered Who this man was. "When the Saviour comes, He will tell us all things," the woman told Jesus.

Quietly Jesus said, "I am He. I am the Saviour God has sent."

The woman left her water jar by the well. She hurried to the town. "Come," she said to the people. "Come, see a man Who has told me wonderful things. He is the Saviour God has sent!"

Many people came with the woman. They wanted to see Jesus and hear what He said. "Stay and tell us more," the people said to Jesus.

Jesus stayed in their town two days. He told them God loved them all. Many people believed He was the Saviour and loved Him. JOHN 4:3-42

Many people came from the town to see Jesus. Who invited them to come and see Jesus? Why did she want the people to see Jesus?

God wants us to tell others about His Son, the Lord Jesus. Who can you invite to go to Sunday School to learn of Jesus? Let's make an invitation and send or take it to a friend.

Thank You, dear God, for sending Your Son Jesus to be our Saviour. Show us how to help our friends learn about Jesus, In Jesus' name.   Amen.   **151**

MADE WELL AGAIN

What do your mother and father do when you are sick?

The Bible tells us about a boy who was very sick. His head hurt and he was hot with fever. His mother and father loved their boy and did everything they could to help him get well. But still he was very sick.

One morning the boy's father said, "I am going to find Jesus. I will ask Him to come and make our boy well."

And the father went as fast as he could to find Jesus. When the father came to the town where Jesus was, he asked, "Where is Jesus? I must talk to Him right away!"

The father hurried through the town until he found Jesus. "My boy is very sick," the father said. "Please, come quickly and make him well!"

Jesus was glad to help. But Jesus did not go with the father. "Your boy is well. He is well now," Jesus said to the father.

The father believed Jesus, and started on his way home. Near home two of his servants came running to him. "Your boy is well!" they shouted. "He is well again!"

Oh how glad the father was! He hurried to the house where the boy and his mother were waiting. Just as the Lord Jesus had said, the boy was well.

How happy they all were in that home. Jesus had made the boy well. Jesus helped because He loved them! They all loved Jesus and believed He was God's Son.

152 JOHN 4:46-53

When the little boy got sick, did his father call a doctor?
What did he do? How did Jesus show He loved the little boy
and the boy's family?

Aren't you glad for a strong, healthy body! Who made you
that way? Do you remember to thank God that you are strong?
You can say or sing this "Thank You" song.

For health and strength and daily food,
We give Thee thanks, O Lord.   Amen.

153

A MAN WHO
WANTED TO WALK

In Bible times there was a man who could not walk. For many days he just sat on his mat and waited beside a pool—a very special pool of water. Sometimes the water in this pool would BUBBLE for just a little while. Then, the lame man would try to get into the bubbling water. He hoped that the bubbling water would make his lame legs well.

One day JESUS came by! But the lame man did not KNOW it was JESUS who stopped right beside him. "Would you like to be made well?" Jesus asked him.

"Oh, YES!" the lame man said. "But when the water bubbles, I have no one to help me get into it." (The lame man STILL did not know that it was the Lord JESUS Who spoke to him!)

"Stand up now!" Jesus said to the lame man. "Pick up your mat and WALK!"

What? WHAT did he hear? And suddenly— the lame man stood up and began to WALK! He was not lame at all! He could walk! (But he STILL did not know it was JESUS Who made him well!)

What a happy man he was! And the first thing he did was WALK to the temple-church to thank God! Soon, along came Jesus to the temple-church. Jesus said to him, "Do what is RIGHT and GOOD!"

This time the man KNEW it was JESUS Who spoke to him. And he really wanted to do as Jesus told him. For he knew that JESUS loved **154** him and made him well.   JOHN 5:1-15

How high can you jump? Aren't you glad for strong legs to run and jump? Can you find anyone in the picture who cannot run and jump? How did Jesus help the lame man?

The lame man was happy that Jesus helped him to be well and strong. He wanted to do what Jesus told him because he loved the Lord Jesus.

Think of ways you can use your strong legs to help someone today.

STORY 77 A PICNIC WITH JESUS

Jesus sat down to rest on a hillside one day. And a great crowd—hundreds and HUNDREDS of people—came to see Him and to hear Him speak. Now Jesus knew that all these people were tired. And they were hungry, too. "Where can we buy food for all these people?" Jesus asked one of His helpers.

"Why, we don't have enough MONEY to buy food for ALL these people!" one of the helpers answered. Just then another helper said, "Here is a boy who has five little biscuits and two fish. But that's not enough food for ALL these people!"

"Oh, but I WANT Jesus to have my lunch!" the boy must have thought. "I DO hope Jesus will take it!" And while the boy was wondering, Jesus already KNEW the special way that HE was going to help.

Then He said to His helpers, "Ask the people to sit down on the grass." And the helpers did! The boy watched and waited to see what Jesus would do.

And THEN—Jesus DID take the lunch! He thanked God. Then He began to break the biscuits and the fish into pieces. The boy could hardly believe what he saw! For there were enough pieces for the helpers to serve ALL those people. And there were twelve baskets FULL of biscuits and fish left over!

What a wonderful picnic that was—when a boy gave his lunch to the Lord Jesus! Just think how Jesus, God's Son, used that boy's little lunch to help ALL those people!   JOHN 6:1-14

Why do you think the little boy in the picture wanted to share his lunch? How do you think the boy knew that Jesus loved him? Do you wish that you could have been the little boy in the picture? Why?

The Lord Jesus always loves and helps you. Do you love Him? Remember this Bible verse, *I love the Lord* (Psalm 116:1).   **157**

EYES MADE TO SEE

Our Bible tells us about a man who had eyes that could not see. He was blind. This blind man sat by the side of a road.

The blind man could feel the warm sun, but he could not see the bright sunlight. He could hear the birds singing and the children laughing, but he could not see them. He could hear his mother and father speak but he could not see them. He could not see anything.

One day the blind man heard step, step, step. Someone stopped near him. Then he felt cool, wet dirt gently placed on his eyes. He heard a kind voice say, "Go to the Pool of Siloam and wash." It was Jesus Who touched his eyes and spoke to him.

Just as Jesus told him to do, the blind man went to the pool and washed the mud from his eyes. Something wonderful happened. "I can see! I can see!" he shouted.

People asked him, "Are you the one who was born blind?"

"Yes, yes, yes! I am the one! But now I can see!" He told everyone he met that Jesus had made his eyes to see.

Another day Jesus talked with this same man again. "Do you believe in God's Son?" Jesus asked him.

"Tell me," the man said, "Who is God's Son? I want to believe in Him."

"I am God's Son," Jesus told him. And right away the man loved and believed in the Lord

158 Jesus. JOHN 9:1-27, 35-38

Shut your eyes. What do you see? Now open them. What do you see? Do you thank God for your eyes?

We are thankful to God for eyes that see so we can work and play, so we can help and show our love to God. Let us tell Him "thank you."

Dear God, we are glad that Jesus loved the blind man and helped him to see. Help us, because we love the Lord Jesus, to use our eyes in ways that help others.

Amen.

TWO THANKFUL SISTERS

One day someone brought sad news to Jesus. "Your friends, Mary and Martha, want you to come right away!" the messenger said to Jesus. "Their brother Lazarus is VERY sick!"

Jesus loved Lazarus and his two sisters and was glad to help them. So Jesus and His helpers started off to the place where Mary and Martha and Lazarus lived.

But Lazarus died before Jesus got there. So Martha hurried to meet Jesus and tell Him Lazarus was dead. "My brother would not have died if YOU had been here!" Martha said to Jesus. "I know YOU are God's Son, and even now YOU can help us!" (Jesus already KNEW how He would help her!)

Soon Mary came down the road to meet Jesus. "My brother would not have died if YOU had been here!" she said. And she began to cry.

How sorry Jesus was that Mary was so sad! (But Jesus already KNEW how He would help!)

"Where have you put Lazarus?" asked Jesus. They showed Him the place where Lazarus' body was. Then they waited. (Jesus already KNEW how He would help them.)

First, He talked to God, His Father in heaven. And then, He called in a loud voice, "Lazarus— come OUT!" And Lazarus CAME! Lazarus was ALIVE! He was WELL!

Oh, how glad Mary and Martha were! Of course, they thanked Jesus many times! And, they even had a special dinner party—just to show **160** Him they loved Him! JOHN 11:1-45; 12:1,2

One day a messenger brought Jesus news from Mary and
Martha. What was it? Why do you suppose they sent this news
to Jesus? When Mary and Martha saw Jesus what did they
tell Him? Jesus knew all about Mary and Martha and Lazarus.
He knew what He would do to help them. Tell what He did.

Jesus knows all about you, too. He knows what is best for
you and will help you. Can you think of ways He helps you?

A GIFT FOR JESUS

Oh, how Mary loved the Lord Jesus! She loved Him because He loved and helped her. Because He was so good and kind. And she loved Him because He made her brother Lazarus well! She loved Him because He helped her know that God always LOVED HER! Oh, how VERY much Mary loved the Lord Jesus!

One day Mary, her sister Martha, and their brother Lazarus invited Jesus to a special dinner party. Martha was busy as can be serving the dinner. But while Jesus and Lazarus and their friends were eating, Mary was thinking—"What CAN I DO to show Jesus I love Him?"

Then, she remembered something! Something very SPECIAL that she could give Him. It was a bottle of lovely PERFUME. Mary was always so careful with it. For this perfume was the most special, and the most PRECIOUS thing she had! And right then, Mary decided, "I will give my PERFUME to the Lord Jesus."

So she went to get the perfume—walked into the room where Jesus was—went to Him—and knelt at His feet. Then, she opened the bottle of PRECIOUS perfume and gave it to the Lord Jesus. She gave Him every BIT of it. She didn't keep ANY for herself! And in every room of the house there was the lovely smell of this precious perfume.

Then Jesus said to all the friends, "Mary has given Me a very wonderful gift!"

And Mary was glad Jesus knew how MUCH she loved Him!

162   JOHN 12:1-3

Why did Mary give Jesus her precious perfume?

When we love someone we want to give him our best gift. Sometimes we make gifts and sometimes we save our money to buy something special. Sometimes the best gift we can give a person is to tell him that we love him. Jesus is glad when we tell Him that we love Him! (Encourage your child to tell Jesus in prayer or by singing that he loves Him.)

LEARNING ABOUT HEAVEN

What busy, glad days Jesus and His helpers had together. They went many places to help people. And Jesus showed the people how very MUCH He loved them. He helped lame people walk. He helped blind people see. And He helped sick people get well again. Oh, those were busy, glad days that Jesus and His helpers had together! And then—Jesus told His helpers He was going away soon!

Going away? Going AWAY? Oh NO! They looked at each other and then they looked at Jesus and they said, "We will go with You!"

For a moment Jesus looked at His helpers. How He loved them! "You cannot go with Me NOW," He said, "but SOME day you can."

Ahhhhhh—not NOW. But SOME day! Then the helpers wanted to know more. So one of them asked Jesus, "Where ARE You going?"

"I am going back to my home in heaven," Jesus answered. "I am going back to live with God, My Father." Then Jesus told them, "I am going to make a home in heaven for YOU—so that you can always be with Me in heaven!" Ahhhhhh—how wonderful!

In heaven there are only GLAD days and HAPPY people. In heaven no one is lame. No one is blind. No one is sick. Ahhhhhh—how WONDERFUL! And do you know what? SOME-DAY all who love the Lord Jesus will live with HIM in heaven! All of God's family will live there forever and ever! The Lord Jesus SAID so!

JOHN 14:1-9

What a wonderful happy place heaven is! Who is there?
Yes, Jesus is there, with God, our loving heavenly Father.

Why did Jesus go back to heaven? Jesus told His friends,
I go to prepare a place (home) *for you* (John 14:2). Someday
all God's family will live with Him in heaven forever. Who can
belong to God's family? All who love the Lord Jesus belong
to God's family. Do you love Him?

SINGING TO JESUS

What a happy day it was! Jesus and His helpers were going to the temple-church in the big city. Jesus was riding on a donkey. Clippety-clop, clippety-clop went the donkey's hoofs along the road. Step, step, step walked Jesus' helpers along the road.

Some people knew that Jesus was coming. Some of them just watched Jesus ride by. But some of them walked along with Him. Then—

MORE people came! Fathers and mothers. Boys and girls. Some even spread their coats in the road to show they wanted Jesus to be their King. Some threw flowers on the road. Some of the people waved palm branches. And SOME ran ahead to tell the other people, "JESUS is coming! JESUS is coming!" Then—

MORE people came to see Jesus. More and MORE people walked along the road. It was almost like a parade. People laughed and sang as they walked along. And children sang their glad songs to the Lord Jesus. "HOSANNA! HOSANNA!" they sang to Him.

Oh, what a happy day this was!

When people in the city heard the singing, they knew that many people were coming. "Jesus is coming! Jesus is coming into the city!" the people were saying. And they ran to meet Him.

Through the city gates and up the street to the temple-church Jesus rode the little donkey. Slowly, Jesus walked up the steps. And there He was glad to hear children singing to Him on this happy day! MATTHEW 21:1-11,15,16

How did the boys and girls long ago tell the Lord Jesus they loved Him when He rode into the city on a donkey? *Hosanna* is a special word of praise to the Lord Jesus. This is the way the children sang their love to Him.

Can you think of a song which praises the Lord? Let's sing it now. Jesus is pleased when we sing glad songs of love to Him.

JESUS DIED FOR OUR SINS

What a happy day it was when Jesus rode on the little donkey into the big city and went to the temple-church. The children sang to Him. The people wanted Him to be their king. But do you know what happened after that happy day?

There came a very sad day. The governor and many other people did not believe Jesus was God's Son. They did not want Him to be their king. They did not love Jesus and did not know that God sent the Lord Jesus to love and help everyone.

The governor told some soldiers to take the Lord Jesus away from the city. On a hillside were two wooden crosses where thieves had been placed to die. The soldiers nailed Jesus on a big wooden cross and put it between the two thieves. And there Jesus was left hanging on the cross to die.

When Jesus died on the cross He took the punishment for all your sins and for all my sins. Do you know why He died and took our punishment? He took our punishment because He loves us. No one but Jesus, God's Son, could love us so much!

Some friends lovingly took Jesus' body and put it in a tomb in a beautiful garden. The tomb was a room made out of stone. Then a great big stone closed the doorway. Jesus' friends went away very sad. They did not understand yet why Jesus died. They had forgotten what Jesus had said

168 would happen. MATTHEW 27:27-60

Why did Jesus die on the cross? Do you believe that He took the punishment for your sins? When you believe this and ask God to forgive your sins (doing or thinking anything wrong, according to God's Word), He forgives your sins and you become His child, a member of God's family.

For God so loved the world, that he gave his only begotten Son, that whosoever believeth in him should not perish, but have everlasting life (John 3:16).

LIVING AGAIN

On the first Easter morning, three women came to the tomb where loving friends had placed Jesus' body. These women were sad, for their wonderful Friend, Jesus, had been put to death.

When the women came near the tomb, they were surprised to see the tomb open. Inside they saw two angels in shining clothes.

"Jesus is not here," the angels told the women. "Jesus is risen, just as He told you. Do you not remember His words?"

Now they remembered Jesus' words. And quickly they ran to tell Jesus' helpers in the city. "Jesus is risen. He is living," they said.

Two of Jesus' helpers wondered about this news that the women told them. As they walked home they talked about the news that Jesus was living.

While they talked, a man quietly came to walk with them. "What things are you talking about," the man asked.

"We are talking about Jesus Who died on a cross," the helpers answered. "Now we hear Jesus is risen."

Then Jesus talked with them about God's promise to send a Saviour Who would die and live again. The helpers listened. They wondered Who this man was.

That evening, Jesus stayed to eat supper with the two helpers. Before He ate, He thanked God for the food. When the helpers heard Him pray, they knew this man was Jesus. Quickly they ran to tell the others that they had seen Jesus, the

170   living Saviour.   LUKE 24:1-32

What were the men talking about as they walked home?
When a Stranger came and walked with them, what did the
Stranger say? How did the men find out it was true?

Jesus reminded the people that God had promised to send a
Saviour Who would die and live again. And that is just what
happened! Jesus was the Saviour—He was alive again!

171

LIVING FOREVER

It was the very first Easter day! But Jesus' helpers were not happy. And His friends were not happy. They were sad, for Jesus was dead.

One of Jesus' friends named Mary Magdalene walked sadly to the garden. There Jesus' body had been laid in a tomb—a special room made out of stone. But when Mary came to the garden—

The tomb was open! The great stone door had been rolled back. "Oooh—someone has taken Jesus' body!" Mary cried. And great big tears filled her eyes.

Then Mary looked inside the tomb. There she saw two ANGELS! "Why are you crying?" they asked her.

"Because I do not know what they have done with the body of the Lord Jesus," Mary answered.

Suddenly, there was Someone standing near Mary. "Why are you crying?" He asked. "Are you looking for someone?"

Mary's eyes were full of tears. "Oh, please," she said, "If YOU have taken Jesus' body, tell me where you have laid Him!" Then—

Gently, He said, "Mary!" Just like that.

The MINUTE Mary heard Him say her name, she KNEW Who THIS man was! He was JESUS! And He was ALIVE!

"Go tell my helpers that I am alive," Jesus said to Mary. And right away Mary DID!

What a wonderful happy day this was when Mary saw Jesus was ALIVE! When she talked with the living Lord Jesus! And that was the very first EASTER day! JOHN 20:11-18

What changed Mary's sadness into gladness? Where do we read that the Lord Jesus is living? Our Bible tells us He is not dead. It says, *He is risen* (Mark 16:6). What does this mean? Yes, it means Jesus is living!

This is the glad Easter news. Easter is a time for gladness and happy singing. Easter is a time for saying, "God, we thank You! Jesus is living!"

BREAKFAST
ON THE BEACH

One night Jesus' helpers got into a boat and went fishing on the lake. They let their big net down-Down-DOWN into the water. And waited. Then they pulled the net UP. But there were no fish in it. The fishermen let the net DOWN again. And waited and waited. They pulled the net UP. Still, no fish.

All night long they were busy putting their net DOWN and pulling it UP again. When morning came, they STILL had caught no fish. The fishermen were tired. And they were HUNGRY.

Then Someone called from the beach! "Have you caught any fish?" (The fishermen didn't know it was JESUS Who called to them.)

"NO-o-o!" they called back.

"Let your net down on the OTHER side of the boat," said Jesus. And the fishermen DID.

THIS time the net was so full of fish they could not even pull it up into the boat. They could only drag it alongside the boat—all the way back to shore!

"Why—it is the Lord JESUS Who called to us!" one of the fishermen said. And when they got back to the beach—sure enough, it WAS Jesus!

And on a little fire nearby, the hungry fishermen saw food cooking! "Come and have your breakfast now," said Jesus. And they DID!

Oh, that food tasted good to those hungry men! They were SO glad Jesus cooked breakfast for them. And they were glad for the fish Jesus helped them to catch. Most of all, they were glad to be

174 with Jesus! JOHN 21:1-13

What did the Lord Jesus do to help the hungry and tired men in the boat? Why did He help them? The Bible says, *The Lord is good to all* (Psalm 145:9). How does the Lord help you? Let's pray this prayer together.

Thank You, dear Lord Jesus, for helping me today.
Thank You, dear Lord Jesus, for loving me always.
Amen.

COMING AGAIN

The two helpers ran to tell the good news to the others. "We have seen Jesus!" they said. "He walked along the road with us. He is living!"

The other helpers listened to the wonderful news! Jesus was not dead. The Lord Jesus was the living Saviour!

And while they were talking, Jesus Himself came into the room. These helpers were surprised. They were even afraid. Then Jesus spoke. "Do not be afraid. It is I," Jesus said. They saw that this really was the living Lord Jesus.

"I must go away for awhile." Jesus said to His helpers.

"Then we will go with You," they said.

"You cannot go with Me now," Jesus answered. "I am going back to get a new home in heaven ready for you. Someday I will come again and we will be together in our heavenly home."

The day came when Jesus was ready to go back to heaven. "Walk with Me out in the country," Jesus said to His helpers. "After I am gone away, you must go all over the world and tell people everywhere that I am the Saviour God sent. Tell them I love them. Tell them God loves them, too. Tell everybody that I am the living Saviour. Tell them I will come back again."

Then, as Jesus spoke to His helpers, something wonderful happened. He began to rise up from the earth. Up, up, up He went until a cloud covered Him and His helpers could not see Him anymore. The helpers remembered that Jesus said,

176 "I will come again." LUKE 24:38-53; JOHN 14:1-6

Jesus' helpers remembered what He told them when He went up in a cloud to heaven. Do you remember what Jesus told them? Jesus wants us to tell everyone what He told His helpers. He said, *I will come again* (John 14:3).

What is Jesus making ready in heaven for all who love Him? Just think—some day Jesus is coming back to earth to take all of His children to their heavenly home!

HAPPY FRIENDS
STORY 88   IN THE TEMPLE-CHURCH

One day Peter and John walked up the hill to worship God at the temple-church. When they came near the gate of the temple, they heard someone calling, "Help me! Please help me!" Peter and John stopped to see who was calling.

They saw a poor man who could not walk. Every day friends carried this lame man to sit by the temple gate. As people passed, they gave the lame man money to buy food and clothes.

When Peter saw the lame man he said, "Look at me." The man looked up and held out his hand. But Peter said, "I do not have money; I have something else. In the name of Jesus Christ, stand up and walk!" Then Peter took the man by the hand and lifted him to his feet. The man stood up! He ran and jumped he was so glad!

The happy man went into the temple-church to praise and thank the Lord God for legs that were well and strong.

"Wasn't this the poor lame man who sat every day by the temple gate?" the people asked when they saw the happy man. "How did his legs become strong enough to walk?"

"Yes, this is the lame man who never walked," said Peter. "But we do not have power to make this man able to walk. Only the Lord Jesus, Who lives in heaven, could make this man able to walk."

The people at the temple listened as Peter told them more about the Lord Jesus. And that day many happy friends at the temple-church believed in the Lord Jesus and loved Him as their

178 Saviour.   ACTS 3:1–4:4

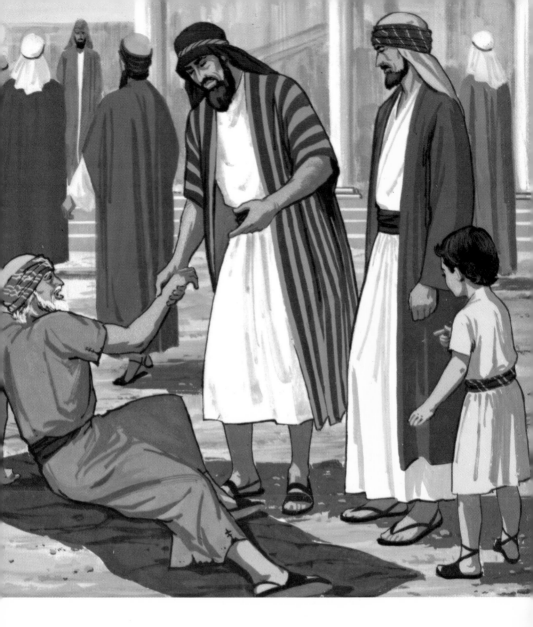

Would you like to tell the story of Peter and John and the lame man? Let's pretend we lived when Peter and John did. Now pretend that you are Peter and/or the lame man. Act out the story and tell what happened.

How did the lame man show his love and thanks to the Lord Jesus? How do you praise and thank the Lord Jesus?

GOOD NEWS IN A CHARIOT

Philip was a Bible time helper who loved the Lord Jesus. He told people the good news about God's Son, the living Saviour.

An angel came to Philip one day with a message from the Lord. "Go and walk on the road in the desert," the angel said to Philip.

On the desert road Philip saw a brightly colored chariot. In the chariot he saw a man from Africa. Philip heard the man in the chariot reading from a Bible scroll.

"Do you understand what you are reading?" Philip asked the man.

"No, I do not understand. I need someone to tell me what this means," the man said. "Can you tell me?"

Philip climbed into the chariot and sat down with the African man. Together they read the Bible scroll about Jesus. Philip told this man about the Lord Jesus, God's own Son.

The African listened and listened. Philip told him the good news that God loved everybody in the world so much that He sent Jesus, His only Son, to be our Saviour.

"If you believe that the living Lord Jesus is God's Son, you are a member of God's family," Philip told his African friend.

"I truly believe that Jesus Christ is God's Son," the man said to Philip. Right then the African man belonged to God's family! The happy man rode back to his home in Africa where he told many, many people the good news about the Lord

180 Jesus Christ. ACTS 8:26-39.

Philip helped a man know and believe in Jesus. Do you know special helpers who tell others about Jesus today?

You can help others know about the Lord Jesus. And you can pray for special helpers who tell others about Jesus— like your Sunday School teacher, your minister, a missionary. Ask God to help them tell others about Jesus—like Philip did.

Let's ask God right now to help each one we have talked about.

GOOD NEWS

STORY 90 **FOR A SOLDIER**

There was a soldier named Cornelius who wanted to hear about Jesus. One afternoon God sent an angel to Cornelius.

"God hears your prayers," the angel told Cornelius. "God wants you to send men to find a man named Peter. They will find Peter in a town called Joppa. Tell your men to bring Peter here to your house. When Peter comes, he will tell you what you should do."

When the angel was gone, Cornelius sent three of his men to find Peter.

The three men went to a town called Joppa. And there they found the man called Peter, just as the angel said.

Now the Lord told Peter that these men were coming; so Peter was waiting. "I am the one you are looking for," Peter said when the three men came. "What do you want?"

The men told Peter about Cornelius. Peter knew that the Lord wanted him to tell Cornelius the good news about the Lord Jesus. So Peter went with the men. Together they walked and walked until they came to Cornelius' house. How glad Cornelius was to have Peter come.

"God loves us all so much that He sent His only Son, the Lord Jesus to be our Saviour," Peter told Cornelius.

Cornelius and all the people in his house listened to this good news. They were glad to know that God sent His only Son, Jesus, to be the Saviour. Now Cornelius and his family loved
182   the Lord Jesus, too.   ACTS 10:1-43.

What good news made Cornelius and his family glad? Do your friends know this good news—that God sent His Son, Jesus, to be our Saviour? Will you tell this good news to your friends?

Who tells you stories about Jesus? Wouldn't it be sad if there were no books like this one—or no Bibles—to help you know and love the Lord Jesus! Let's thank God for the Lord Jesus Christ and for the Bible.

GOOD NEWS
FROM A PRISONER

Peter traveled many places to tell about the Lord Jesus. Some people were glad to hear Peter tell them the good news of the Lord Jesus. But King Herod was not glad about the good news of the Lord Jesus. He thought he could stop Peter from telling about Jesus. He had his soldiers put Peter in a dark prison.

Peter's friends were sad when they learned he was in prison. Every day they met together and prayed for Peter.

One night these friends were praying at a house in the city. Peter was in prison sound asleep. The soldiers were sleeping, too. God sent an angel to the prison. The angel touched Peter and said, "Get up quickly." The chains dropped from Peter's hands. But the soldiers did not wake up.

"Put on your shoes and coat and follow me," the angel said to Peter. Peter obeyed.

Past all the sleeping soldiers Peter followed the angel. The big heavy prison gate opened wide for them. The angel walked down a street in the city. Peter followed. Then suddenly the angel was gone.

Peter hurried to the house where his friends were praying for him. When the friends opened the door, there stood Peter.

"How did you get here?" they asked. Peter told them God sent an angel to take him from prison. And Peter went many places to tell the good news that God loves us and sent His Son to **184** be our Saviour. ACTS 12:1-17.

What good news about Jesus did Peter tell many people? All of us can tell others about Jesus. Who do you know that tells other people about Jesus?

Can you tell others about Jesus? What good news about Jesus can you tell your friends?

TELLING THE GOOD NEWS

One day the Lord Jesus spoke to a man named Paul. "Go tell everyone about Me," Jesus said. So Paul went to big cities and to little towns. He went to nearby places and to faraway places. Everywhere Paul told what the Lord had done for him. Oh, how he loved the Lord Jesus!

Paul told the people, "The Lord LOVES you! He sent the Lord Jesus to be your wonderful Saviour. Now He is living in heaven!"

Some people did not want Paul to talk about the Lord Jesus. They asked the governor to keep Paul in prison. But that did not stop Paul. For in the prison Paul told the prisoners and the guards about the Lord Jesus.

One day the king and his sister came to hear Paul at the governor's big house. Everyone wore fine clothes. Soldiers with shining helmets came with their long spears. It was like a parade.

Then Paul came in with heavy chains on his arms from the prison. Paul could hardly wait to tell of the wonderful things the Lord Jesus had done for him. Finally the king said, "We are ready to hear you now." And Paul gladly told about the Lord Jesus Who came to be their wonderful Saviour and Friend.

When Paul was finished, he said, "O King, I pray that you, and all these people here, will someday know and love the Lord Jesus, too."

The governor and the king then decided Paul should go to faraway Rome. And Paul was glad! For there he could tell MORE people of the

186   Lord Jesus!   ACTS 25:13-27; 26

What does Paul have on his arms in the picture? Why was Paul put in prison? Who told Paul to tell everyone about the Lord Jesus. The Bible says, *Tell . . . great things the Lord hath done* (Mark 5:19). What great things did Paul want to tell everyone about the Lord Jesus? What did he tell the king? What can you tell your friends about the Lord Jesus?

187

TELLING NEW FRIENDS

One day the governor sent Paul on a long trip. Paul went with soldiers and sailors and other travelers in a big sailing ship. Paul must have had a GOOD time telling them of the Lord Jesus!

Out on the ocean the little waves became BIG waves. The gentle winds became STRONG winds. The sailing ship was tipped and turned about. And finally, the winds and the waves pushed the ship right into the land. The ship broke all to pieces! But all the people got to land safely.

The people who lived on the land came to help the cold and wet people from the broken ship. And the chief of the land invited Paul to stay at his house.

Paul soon learned that the chief and his people did not know and love the Lord Jesus. What a GOOD time Paul must have had telling them God loved them, and sent the Lord Jesus to be their wonderful Saviour and dear Friend.

One day Paul visited the chief's sick father. Paul prayed for him. Right then, the Lord did a wonderful thing. He made the father well!

Paul prayed for other sick people. And the Lord made many others well, too! Paul was SO glad he could tell these new friends about the Lord Jesus Who loved them and had made them well!

Soon it was time for Paul to go on with his long trip. Paul was a glad traveler. For he was on his way again to another land. And there he could tell others great and wonderful things the

188 Lord has done. ACTS 27–28:11

Where did the governor send Paul? What happened on the trip? Did the people know about the Lord Jesus? Paul told them of *great things the Lord hath done.* When he stayed at the chief's house the Lord did a wonderful thing. What was it? Paul was so glad he told the people about the Lord Jesus.

Dear God, we are glad that You love us. Help us to tell our friends that You love them, too. In Jesus' name.   Amen.

READY TO
TELL GOOD NEWS

In Bible times there lived a boy named Timothy. Timothy's mother and his grandmother told him Bible stories over and over again.

Sometimes Timothy would sit by his grandmother while she talked to him. Do you suppose Timothy had a favorite Bible story—like you do? Maybe his grandmother told him the story of how God took care of Baby Moses. Or about Jacob who went on a long trip by himself.

When Timothy was just your age he began to learn some of the same Bible verses that you know —like, *Make a joyful noise unto the Lord, all ye lands. Serve the Lord with gladness* (Psalm 100:1, 2).

Timothy's mother and his grandmother helped Timothy know the good news about Jesus. They helped Timothy know and love God's Son, Jesus.

Timothy grew stronger and taller. He learned to read the Bible scrolls. Timothy grew to be a man who loved the Lord Jesus.

One day a missionary came to the city where Timothy lived. His name was Paul. Paul needed a good helper who loved the Lord Jesus. He needed someone who knew and loved God's Word. Paul was glad to find a young man like Timothy to help him tell the good news about Jesus.

Timothy's mother and his grandmother must have been very glad that Timothy could go with Paul. They remembered to pray that Timothy would be a good helper, and that Timothy would help people know and love the Lord Jesus, God's

190 Son.   ACTS 16:1-8; II TIMOTHY 1:5; 3:14-16.

How did Timothy know what God's Word said? Do you suppose he had a favorite Bible story? Perhaps he learned some of the same Bible verses you know, such as *I will not forget thy word* (Psalm 119:16).

When Timothy grew to be a man, what did he do? Listening and learning God's Word helped him to tell others about God. Aren't you glad for people who tell you about God?

LETTERS OF GOOD NEWS

In Bible times Paul wrote letters to people in the city of Rome. Paul wrote to tell these people the good news about Jesus. God helped Paul know what to write. Paul's letters told them that God loved them all so much that He sent His Son Jesus to be their Saviour.

Then one day Paul took a trip. He went on a big ship to the city of Rome. In Rome the Christians often came to Paul's house. The Christians loved the Lord Jesus and they wanted to hear Paul tell them more about Jesus, their Saviour. Sometimes people who did not know and love the Lord Jesus came to Paul's house. He was glad to tell them of Jesus, God's Son.

One day a poor, frightened man named Onesimus came running to Paul's house. Onesimus was in trouble. He had run away from his master, the man for whom he worked. Paul asked Onesimus to stay with him. There, at Paul's house, Onesimus heard the good news about the Lord Jesus.

Onesimus knew he should go back to work for his master. So Paul wrote a letter for Onesimus to give the master. Paul's letter asked the master to be kind and let Onesimus work for him again.

Then Onesimus said goodbye to his friend Paul. How glad Onesimus must have been for that good letter he was taking from Paul to his master!

Paul wrote many letters of good news about the Lord Jesus. God helped Paul know what to write in these letters. In our Bible we can read the letters Paul wrote. ACTS 28:11-31;

PHILIPPIANS 1:13; II TIMOTHY 4:7; PHILEMON.

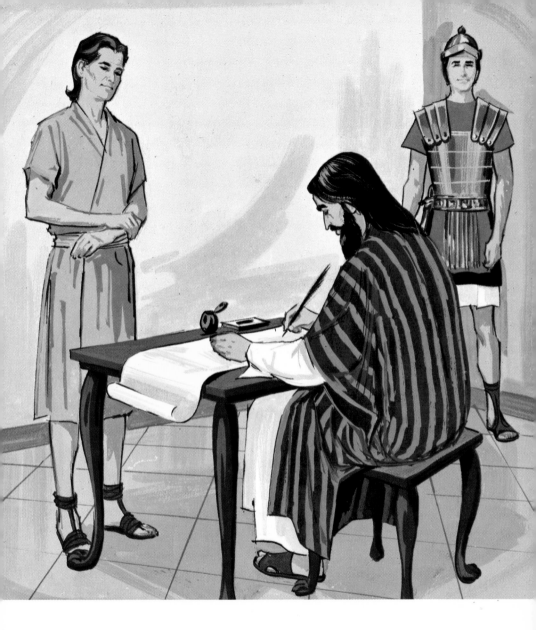

In this story how did Paul help people to know and love the Lord Jesus? After Onesimus listened to Paul tell about Jesus, what did Onesimus decide to do?

Where can we read the letters Paul wrote to tell others about Jesus? Can you help write a letter to tell others about Jesus?

GOOD NEWS FROM AN ISLAND

In Bible times John was one of Jesus' special helpers. John liked to be with Jesus and talk with Him. And John told many people the good news about the Lord Jesus. John also wrote what he heard Jesus say.

When John was an old man, he went to live on an island. One day on the island, John heard a voice saying, "Write in a book the things you see. Then send what you write to the people who love Me."

It was the Lord Jesus talking to John. "I will show you what to write," Jesus said. Then He showed John many wonderful things in heaven.

John saw that heaven is a beautiful, happy place. There is no nighttime in heaven. There is no sickness or sadness. And no one ever gets hurt in heaven. Everyone is truly happy in heaven.

John saw the Book of Life. The Book of Life is a wonderful book in heaven. In this Book are written the names of every person who loves the Lord Jesus. But more wonderful than all else, John saw the Lord Jesus in heaven!

When Jesus had shown John many wonderful things in heaven, John heard the Lord say, "Write what you have seen so all may know these things I have shown you."

For many, many days John carefully wrote on his long scrolls, just as the Lord Jesus told him. In our Bible we can read the words the Lord Jesus told John to write.

194   REVELATION 1; 21:3,23,25,27; 22:5,10,16.

What did the Lord Jesus tell John to do? Why did Jesus want John to write about what he saw? John saw a wonderful Book of Life in heaven. What is in this Book? Is your name there? Everyone whose name is in the Book will live in heaven forever.

Thank You, dear God, for the Bible that says those who love the Lord Jesus will be with Him in heaven.

Amen.